DIVIDED WE FALL

A Guide for the Modern Patriot

BY:

JOEY BRUNO

PLANET 20
PRODUCTIONS

Divided We Fall – A Guide for the Modern Patriot
Written by: Joey Bruno

For bulk and discount purchases of this title for your group or organization please contact: admin@modernpatriots.com

The author is available for public speaking on this subject as well as appearances for book promotion please contact Joey Bruno by emailing: joey@modernpatriots.com

isbn – 1448664519

ean-13   9781448664511

Dedication

This book is dedicated to all those, throughout the world and throughout time, who have fought for liberty – either for themselves or for others.

Our hearts are with you and we owe you our deepest gratitude.

The purpose of this book is to keep your extraordinary efforts and your fire alive, to spark it within those who have yet to recognize it and to rekindle it in others who may have felt it fade.

Thank you and God bless you for your sacrifices.

We will never forget...

Acknowledgments

It is impossible to take on a task such as writing a book without the help of others. Whether it be through their willing effort or unintentional inspiration is unimportant – it still takes a small army to get the job done.

To my dear close friends, either in my tangible, tactile life or online – I truly value your opinions, input and encouragement during this process. Your thoughts, feelings and personal insight are more valuable than gold. As many who know me will attest, we don't have to agree on a point for me to know that your opinion is priceless – because it is a God given gift and a valuable right to be able to freely express one's thoughts.

For those who are honest in the media – Thank you for slugging it out each day and for doing what you do. The passive reader or listener has no idea the great amount of heavy lifting it takes to do what you do. Between prep., fact checking and production, you have quite an impossible task every day. All the audience or reader knows (and enjoys) is a silky smooth finished product as they ingest it and wait for the next installment. Your voice is vital. Thank you!

To my dear reader. Thank you for being a Patriot. In the early days of this country publications like this one weren't so rare. The personal and social enslavement (that's a fair description) of the colonists by England was rampant and great. Brave and wise men took it upon themselves, risking personal harm or imprisonment, to write books and pamphlets calling for the unity of the people to fight tyranny and strive for their liberty.

In essence, this makes us the founders of a rediscovered spirit of hope in this country and for the reawakening of personal liberty. Not an easy task – but the price of liberty and freedom requires effort and a drive forward for the benefit of all – whether they follow in your footsteps or not. By simply having and reading this book you are making the conscious effort to do something. That in itself is both empowering and inspiring.

So, while you may not have taken an active role in the writing of this book, your participation by reading it completes the cycle and allows my efforts to enjoy their destiny.

To those that said they would never read this book, I say welcome. There are many (for outward social or political reasons) who have wished me "much luck" with the book, but reminded me that they will never crack open the cover.

I still welcome them inside.

Because, who can blame them? Many suffer from a fatigue in believing that this book will parrot the same rhetoric they have heard a thousand times before. That it will contain finger pointing and possibly attack their way of thinking. Not this book.

If you read further you will quickly discover that a true patriot has no allegiance to party or politics. His (or her) allegiance is to his fellow man and their common rights and liberties as a people. Hopefully they will discover that what they've wrongly been led to believe by others, has no home or voice in this book.

Within these pages I wish to offer hope to us all. A renewed sense of oneness throughout our core as the greatest people and country on earth.

We are Americans.

Table of Contents

FOREWORD

Divided We Fall
A Guide for the Modern Patriot

by:
Joey Bruno

FOREWORD

I love America.

I love it's people, the scenery, apple pie, classic cars, it's history, American movies, our space program, MOTOWN, Elvis, Corvettes, the best golf anywhere, hot dogs, little kids, our beaches, Texas, The Statue of Liberty, Microsoft, Apple Computers, Highway 101, Jack Daniels, Our Flag, Tabasco, Boeing, NASCAR, College Football, KODAK, Band Aids, Ford, fishing, old folks, talk radio, John Wayne, Captain Kirk, Pee-Wee Herman, Roy Orbison, Mickey Mouse, bowling, Hershey's, Aretha Franklin, target shooting, S.U.V.'s, parades, fireworks, pretty girls, cable television, God above!, bikinis, body builders, laundromats, bean bag chairs, the Grand Canyon, Cessna airplanes, Universal Studios, The Fox News Network, SPAM (in a can), Carson, Las Vegas, our forests, our military, firemen, cops and anyone tough enough to wear a uniform – including milkmen, sprinklers, the telephone, the moon landings, The Andy Griffith Show, Goodyear, Main Street, Ansel Adams, cold beer, Kona Coffee, baseball, "Silly String" and fried chicken.

The list goes on.

Is that your version of America? It is for me – maybe you have your own – but it's still the same beautiful America. There's so much going on today in our country, there have been problems with the economy, power grabs in Washington D.C. and it seems, sadly, that the best our public servants can do is write a larger I.O.U. to the system and then send us the bill as the answer to everything that faces us.

I watch this and I ponder, I've given this a great deal of thought. I'm a reasonably intelligent guy and I can do math with the best of them.

The majority of these so called "answers" just don't hold up to rational, common sense. Simple as that.

I have a very firm grasp in my head as to the causes of the current economic crunch this nation suffers from. I understand the AIG situation, TARP money, the Bush Administration thrusting a bailout upon Wall Street and the Congressional votes and twisting of Fannie Mae and Freddie Mac for "special interest" favoritism (disguised as economic stimulus) that started the whole mess to begin with. I understand the Obama White House and a Democratic Congress making their political power moves and striking while the iron is hot.

Can I draw on this knowledge and those points over a beer and make powerful argument when the conversation turns to "politics"? You bet I can.

But most folks can't.

I used to just sit there, listening to others spout public opinion points, vent their emotions and watch them become highly agitated during these conversations. Literally taking offense to me and my argument because it was so straightforward and factual and that it didn't fracture into a million little "social" issues and arguments.

Labeled as an insensitive "bully" we would both go our separate ways, each muttering "idiot" concerning the other.

I didn't want to argue with them. I wanted them to see that they were all hyped up over nothing. I offered facts and references where they could check what I was saying. I wasn't trying to deceive them or sway them. I was trying to get us both on the same page.

The aggravation of this drove me crazy. People, some that I liked and cared about, were just running around (in my opinion) in a fog. They were unwilling to look at the big picture. Which I must admit, was so big that at times it was difficult for someone even like myself, who followed the issues and studied the facts, to see.

Still, I couldn't for the life of me understand how so many people can be so animated over things that they clearly had no real knowledge of. They just knew that certain issues effected them and they had strong "feelings" about it...

...and that's just it – that's all they knew.

This bothered me on a deep level. I take time out of my life to see what's happening on Capitol Hill and, believe it or not, I'm not a fan of politics. I don't bide my time watching or listening to every political show that comes on. The main thing is that I just like to keep current in my world.

But there was some - "thing" that really got under my skin about folks who would whine (at great volume) about those "damn politicians" and not have the first inkling or knowledge on the subject at hand. Just exercising their First Amendment right to "gripe" with no substance or facts to their arguments whatsoever. They had their "feelings" and "passion" and that, to them, was enough.

It's clear to me that griping begets griping. Birds of a feather so to speak. The clear danger, I have learned, is that most people who are animated on a subject, that have no facts, are always the ones expecting someone else to fix a problem. Clearly, they are too busy to worry with anything as mundane as finding an answer, they just want it fixed.... magically fixed.

But, gripe as they may, we never see any real solutions appear.

What about the "problem fixers" that these people were referring to in all of their arguments – you know, those "damn politicians"?

I gave that some though too and I finally realized that they weren't truly trying to solve any problems at all. Politicians are simply working on their careers.

Bureaucrats say things all the time about them doing what the "people" want – but I'm still trying to find this majority of people they're always talking about. Truth is, if they were handling things that were truly right and just by the American people there wouldn't be all of these folks whining about everything and going on about how the Politicians are failing them..

This is what laid on my mind a very long time. These two ideas grated against each other in my brain like fingernails on a chalkboard. (Believe me, once that's in your head – you won't like it.)

At first I tried to find a "balance" between these two points. Maybe the citizens needed to take the time to brush up their knowledge of things a little and the politicians needed to spend more time working alongside the "common man" and discover more about their issues and needs.

That worked in my thoughts for a while, at least it got that screeching sound down to a manageable hum. But every so often something would happen and that awful sound would spike a little in my head.

No, this wasn't an answer, it was a compromise and actually it's the same old compromise that we've been using for a long time.

My mind was trying to settle for the same old dysfunctional answers. We are creatures of habit and try as we might to be creative about a solution, it's very difficult to ask our brains to leap somewhere that they've never been. As clever as I pride myself on being – the frustration continued.

People just won't take the time to study the actual problems, at least the majority of them won't. There are some really great talk radio hosts busting their chops everyday spitting out facts that you can look up for yourself... and people either repel them and won't listen or they never take the time or pick up the yoke and investigate these points on their own.

Politicians pour money (our money) all over little projects everywhere to quiet and comfort the people and their issues – but it's never enough. The want and need from an apathetic and seemingly mindless voting public just continues to grow.

Constantly... and as long as they're promising something and re-wetting the pacifier – most people just go back to their grumblings and continue to tough it out.

It doesn't work.

There had to be an answer. A real answer.

Then it came to me. Simple, quiet, basic. Like a whisper in the wind from an angel. The answer was simple – so very, very simple.

By pure luck I ran across a copy of a book called "The Business Encyclopedia". It's an old book, and has been out of print for quite a while now. My copy is dated 1949. It was edited by Henry Marshall and published by Doubleday.

This fragile, 60 plus year old book is a dream come true for a guy like me. I love business and this little gem is a historical account of all things business related from back in those days.

This single hard cover book, at 515 pages contains examples of business contracts, charts, tables, even the proper design of business cards and letters of correspondence. These were the days well before FAX machines, cell phones, copiers and computers.

I was fascinated by the simple elegance of everything within it.

Contracts, deeds, accountancy.... so much more streamlined and efficient because those methods simply worked. Thumbing and reading through it at random (I rarely read a reference book, in order, from cover to cover) I discovered something within it, starting around page 94 of the book, that took me by total surprise.

There, in black and white was a description of the functions and departments (branches) of the United States Government. The pages that followed also contained the entirety of the U.S. Constitution and all of the amendments (up until that time).

I was floored.

The Constitution in a business book? A thorough business book, that was clearly a standard, at that!

Why in the world would they have a copy of the Constitution within a book about business?

In 1949 businesses recognized the proper role of Government in protecting the free market and how important it was for the Government to support business in order to keep the economy and, ultimately, the United States strong. So, powerful business men made it their duty to know and understand the workings and the function of the U.S. Constitution and the Government.

I'm ashamed to admit that in all of my years I had never taken the time to actually read the most important government document in the world. Well, it's right here in front of me. I may as well take advantage of this. I braced myself for a struggle – just waiting to be tangled up in a bunch of legal speak and "government" style mish-mash. I sat down to read it.

I was delightfully amazed.

A child can read this thing! I read it from top to bottom (taking my time to make sure that I was clear on every point) and it took a whopping forty minutes from my life.

After I finished it, I remember sitting there stunned for many minutes. It was like someone telling you that you were born on a different planet and that this is not your home world. I thought about what I had just read. The simplicity. The clarity.

I had just been initiated into the Constitutional "reality club".

I looked at the world around me in a new light. Uplifted and hopeful from the purity I had just read.

Then the realization of of my country's current status crept back in.

I finally summoned the courage to ask myself, "How did this mess happen?"

The truth is, there is no way that we built the nation we have today upon the shoulders of a document so pure and simple that is dedicated to the freedoms and liberties of people. Impossible. The Constitution still exists, no doubt, but we surely don't have the messes that we do today because of following it's guiding principles and instructions. Again, impossible.

Somewhere, along the way, things have been intentionally twisted and maligned and clearly not for the good of the people. Knowing now, what the people were missing, it was clear to me that it wasn't the "people" who were orchestrating this. There is no way that anyone would every willingly, knowingly or intentionally surrender the liberties guaranteed in this document.

I dug all into this subject. The history, congressional records, political and world events... What was the trail that got us here? It was so twisted, contrived and slow that the erosion process reminded me of the lazy and serene waters that had carved the beautiful Grand Canyon over time.

This was insane as well as criminal. The American public, for the most part, have no clue whatsoever as to what and where they could and would be today if their rights and freedoms hadn't been infringed upon over all these years. I was beside myself.

With a hot passion I grabbed my trusty word processor and I pounded away writing pages with a fury and spirit I had never possessed.

Then I realized, the moment of truth....

… that I was wrong.

I was finger pointing and in doing so, I sounded like all the usual pundits in the world of politics. Then I flashed back to the many political conversations I've had with others.

I was just a guy trying to make a point. A point that was going to fall on deaf ears. Right as rain mind you, but what I was writing was nothing new. Frustrated, dejected and honestly, pretty ticked at myself, I put it down.

I knew that my arguments, although correct, were old. Many folks already know what I now knew and they preach it constantly to no avail.

You see, having a point and being right about it means nothing if people can't grasp it or won't take the time to listen and learn.

No, it had to be simpler, more basic to the heart of the matter within the confines of a simpler and greater commonality. Something, like the Constitution. Something for everyone, the people... We the People.

That was it!

We needed a handbook! A simple little publication like those written in the days of the colonists. A book that explains liberty and how it impacts everyone, not the few elitists like we have now, but a common book for the common man! It would briefly talk of the broad problems, define both our role and the politicians role in those problem and provide a simple, unified solution.

This is what you hold in your hands.

"Divided We Fall" is all about keeping it simple. It's about looking at the world around us without having to get involved with all the myriad complexities of the "politics" surrounding the issues.

This isn't a book for Conservatives or Liberals, this book is for Americans. The people. Men and women like yourself. This book is color and religion blind, it's totally neutral, because in all of us lies the core – the core of the American spirit. We're all neighbors, we're all family, and we have a bond – a bond that's hard to see with all of our "special interests" piled on top of it – but a powerful core bond all the same.

I've been to a few patriotic events and I'm here to tell you, when you're thinking "red, white and blue" you can't see peoples' skin color or think about what religion they are. You don't think about whether they belong to a Union or their personal status and wealth. You only see people. People who care about your liberties, their liberties and love their country... and that bond.

That's what we need to understand, nurture and grow.

We need to regain our center. Get in touch with our commonality as Americans. It's the only way. We must find the strength and courage to strip it all down to the core.

That's our simple answer.

Let's find our center, understand our power and authority (as guaranteed in the Constitution), keep it simple and act on it.

With a basic, simple common vision and understanding of these principles you're eyes will open and you'll be able to smell a politician trying to be "clever" from a mile a way.

Want your country back? I do. Like I said, I love America – all of it.

Today, we start our journey. Not as newly invented Democrats or Republicans, Conservatives or Liberals, but as Patriots. True American Patriots.

CHAPTER

1

We're In a Mess...

I don't care what political party you subscribe to. I don't care if you're a liberal or a conservative or maybe an independent. I don't care if you're one of those hyphenated Americans (African-American, Italian-American, Irish-American, etc.), a member of a Labor Union, Atheist, White Collar worker or a Homosexual... I simply don't care.

Just stop for a minute and quit worrying about saving the Rain Forests or the the environment. Stop whining over who's gonna benefit from this, that or the other thing and just get still.

Be still.

Breathe in slowly.... and exhale.

Get still and clear your mind. Just listen to what I have to say. Don't try and read between the lines (I'm not that clever of a writer) and just take the actual words in for their face value.

Ready?

We're in trouble. Major, major trouble. The core of our country is dying. Our fabric as a nation is being destroyed and we have to do something about it. Stopping this and fixing this is more important than anything in the world. Yes, I said it, in the world.

We are citizens of the United States of America. The world depends on us, our charity, our benevolence, our stewardship and mostly, our liberty. Without us, a unified American people, this world will starve, go bankrupt and blast itself into a trillion pieces.

We have, as a people, been asleep at the wheel, worrying about our day to day tasks and our little issues for so long that our apathy has made us the laughing stock and "whipping boy" of the world.

Our dollar is shrinking on the world markets. The majority of Europe (whom we saved in 2 world wars) spits out our name in detest when they mention us. The middle east defies our efforts for peace and would just as soon terrorize us at every turn. China (who basically owns us), North Korea and the Soviet Union could care less about us and wished that we weren't in their way of a wanted world domination. The U.N. (while a joke) enjoys a world headquarters in our country and squelches us at every turn.

To top it off? We have a bureaucratic machine, alive and well in Washington D.C. and it's growing like a cancer. The people (politicians) in it don't give a care about what you think, say or do – so long as they get to stay in office and keep their ever growing power alive. These politicians, and their hijacking of our freedoms and liberties, not the U.S. Government, are the seat of all these problems.

End of story.

We the people, have done it to ourselves and have only ourselves to blame. Not the News Networks, the Politicians, or the self appointed "social leaders" – but ourselves. I'm not just referring to the person in your mirror – I mean your neighbors too. The person who waves as they cut their grass, your pastor, your best friend, your parents, your child's teacher, your dentist – all guilty. They've either been apathetic and just let it all slip or they've been aware of the situation – and didn't do anything or enough to stop it.

But the sad, heart wrenching fact is that we, all of us, did it to ourselves.

Let that fact soak in for a second.

Every gripe you have about the government is self inflicted. Are they wasting too many tax dollars? Your fault. Do you feel that they are taking away too many of your freedoms or liberties? Your fault. Don't like how we are being treated or looked upon worldwide? Also your fault. It is all of our collective fault.

Why?

Because we (as a people) allowed it.

This great country was not founded on the idea that the government was to be in charge of everything, or even us. It, and our government leaders weren't supposed to do anything except our bidding. Our collective, rational, freedom loving, self responsible, decent, reasonable, bidding.

The United States Government was designed to act as a glue, controlled by the U.S. Constitution and given power by the people to guide and protect the collective states with management and protection when the need arose. Hence our name, The *United* States of America.

Our founding fathers and the framers of the Constitution were very keen on the dangers of a government growing too large and out of control. When they drafted and finally made official the Constitution they included several mechanisms within it to help prevent this, but mostly, they were adamant on the concept that the government be the servant of the people.

The idea was that the people would control the government and that they (the people) would give it (the government) power and authority. The original, and still functional design in no way resembles the perverted and convoluted system that is currently working on Capitol Hill today. (That we follow blindly as a programmed social habit.)

So, the next time you're mad that the Government because it's wasting your tax money, is running a terrible deficit and budget or you see someone on welfare driving a new Lexus – rather than gripe – go to your nearest mirror and say, "Thank you! Job well done!". For that matter, go and hug your neighbor and you can congratulate each other for your collective efforts. We allowed this to happen and we did it together.

How in the world did we get from there to here? How did we start with a Constitution that kept government to a minimum and end up with huge life sucking monster like our current bureaucratic system? One piece at a time.

We did it slowly by voting people into offices who promised to grant us and our little self interest, a "favor".

"If elected, I promise to _____ and to support that effort without fail!"

(Fill in the blank with whatever it is that you personally like. For instance – Free Beer on Fridays, half off of accessories with any purchase of a hand bag , etc.)

Then people who had an interest in that subject voted for them based on that promise.

Of course, for your politician to do these things and to fulfill those promises, it takes money. Yet there's only (in theory) so much of that to go around. So you have to tax more in order to fulfill those "special interest" campaign promises.

Your elected politician can't just appropriate and throw the peoples' money around for any reason. It has to be brought up, voted on and approved. (This is basically how things *should* work) But.... if you are a politician and your constituents in congress (or elsewhere) don't see the need to support that particular promise to your voters - then you have to scratch someones back.

Scratch it long enough so the next time a new law is written, maybe concerning Automobile Safety, some freshly scratched fellow congressperson with some pull will get your "Free Beer on Friday" money included, with this new and separate law, as a little bonus. Now, multiply this times every elected official wanting a little "goodie" hidden away or worse, something buried that helps them maintain their authority and office – and "we" have a huge problem.

To the politicians it's a win/win! They get to play "hero" *and* gloat over their brilliance. In our example we get Free Beer *and* Safer Cars all at the same time! Thank you Uncle Sam! You're a godsend!

All the while nothing is being done with a true consensus of the peoples' real collective needs and everything is slanted and twisted with a political flair.

As ludicrous as that example is, that's pretty much how it all works. It's snowballed from there, with more intertwining of laws, debt through the roof, power grabbing, vote pandering and the trimming of American liberties. It shows no sign of slowing down and just keeps getting worse.

This is a very simplified example and all of the ins and outs of it are very complex – but suffice it to say – the U.S. Constitution was not designed to support the idea of a free thinking "Career Politician". Sadly, that's the only kind there is and that practice is killing us as a nation.

Politicians are no longer our public servants, doing our bidding and "guiding" this nation. They are "running" it as they choose, bending constitutional mandate and doing it all in the name of what's good for the people. Whether you're willing to recognize it or not, we are the fuel and lubricant for their power machine. As a people, we have no choice but to stop it!

Yes, we're in trouble. You know it, I know it, and the politicians revel in it.

This stirring up of special interest issues and finger pointing between the parties (and the people) is nothing more than a smoke screen so that you and I won't notice what's going on behind the curtain (a la "Wizard of Oz"). They are manipulating us at every turn and the more we grumble amongst ourselves, the more they gain and benefit.

The very idea that the American public might just stop and be still, as I suggested at the beginning of this chapter, and study their movements terrorizes them to no end. Yet, they live comfortably day to day knowing how self absorbed you are with your little life or that you are so dependent upon "big brother" that you wouldn't dare bite the hand that feeds you. No, don't fool yourself, America politicians rest easily at night knowing that you don't dare take your precious time to watch them with scrutiny.

It's time we did.

Surely, we have failed ourselves as a people. We have failed each other as neighbors and friends. Life is tough and we all make mistakes. But no matter how simple or damning the mistake is, there is only one way to fix it.

We must learn to be better citizens as a nation by establishing a core set of beliefs about our liberties and the value of them. We must make it our business to know how the Constitution and how government works so we can understand how they are both used against us. Develop a good "nose" for politicians who try and manipulate us in order to "buy" our vote or be wise to them as they try and "sell" us a new program that's a "power extender" disguised as something else. Be on alert, vote wisely and vow to never let our loss of government control happen again!

The toughest part? We each must take personal responsibility for what's gone wrong.

We are going to have to do some soul searching, get still and find our center and realize that we (each of us) are the largest part of the problem. Realize that there are far more people in the public than there are holding office in Washington D.C.

We sent them there and we have let our control and monitoring of them and their actions slip. They are out of control.

Find your mirror, have a good heart to heart with yourself and be honest.

Now, go and be honest with your neighbor. Don't chew on your words either. Tell them your heart. Tell them your revelation. Tell them the truth.

Tell them that you have thought about it sincerely and you feel terrible about. Tell them that you owe them an apology. Then apologize. Let them take that thought with them, after their soul searching, they may share the same with others. That honesty and that truth will grow. Because each of us owe each other a terribly over due apology.

So, for the record, to all of you, I apologize.

I've made a terrible mistake and it's my fault.

I'm not happy with the America I see today. I've done my fair share of griping about it – but I was wrong to do that – because it's my fault.

I gave my government more authority and control than it could handle. I've helped elect people whose power went to their head. I saw it, knew it and I did nothing about it.

I give you my word, that I'm sorry that I let myself and you (my fellow Americans') down and I'm taking the steps to correct this problem so that it never happens to me or any of us again.

That's my apology and my pledge to you.

Will you do the same one for me?

CHAPTER

2

What does it mean to be an American?

Personally, I can't stand the food at McDonald's. Truth is, I can't find anyone (over the age of – I dunno – maybe 12) who can actually stomach the stuff. The service is poor, the facilities are never quite, um... pristine and honestly, their offerings just by the slimmest definitions can be passed off as "food".

Doesn't stop me from dragging into their drive through at midnight for a large fries and a coke! (It's a guilty pleasure....)

But, there it is – like it or not, McDonald's is alive and well and it is quite a thriving institution.

Wonder how that is, with a society as clearly overweight as ours is and as un-"heart-healthy" as their food can be – what

keeps the Golden Arches chugging along? I'll tell you –
consistency.

Face it, no matter where you go in this land, you'll find a
McDonald's and that same hum-drum cheeseburger you get in
Philadelphia will be the exact same size, shape, quality and
taste as the one in Tacoma. I mean identical!

So, when you're cruising down the road and are hungry, as
yucky as it is, everyone in the car will surrender and agree on
McDonald's. May not be great, may not be what you want, but
you know without fail exactly what you're going to get.
Crappy and Consistent.

This is what we've allowed ourselves to become in this
country. Crappy and consistent. We deal with each other that
way on a personal and social level and we allow ourselves to
be treated that way from our own government. We even go a
step further. When Washington D.C. does something "crappy
and consistent" we all just shrug it off. We might gripe about it
for a day or two at the water cooler but, ultimately we relent
and just give it a pass.

After all, it's what we've come to expect.

JOEY'S LIFE – Scene 2,624,994

INTERIOR –   CAR OF LIFE – GOING DOWN LIFE'S
             HIGHWAY – CONGRESS DRIVING

CONGRESS: LILTING, LIKE A HAPPY MOM

           **"Okay, we're pulling in to a McDonald's –
           what do you want?"**

ME: THINKING (Aww crap – I hate this place.....)
           SHRUGS, MUMBLES
           "I dunno – a cheeseburger.."

Later, while I'm choking down my little burger in the back seat, I can get back to my comic books, my IPOD and put my mind on other "important" things. Dry and chewy as it was, and bought with my own money, at least I'm not hungry anymore.

Take a long look at us. Why are we content with this mindset? "Crappy and Consistent" indeed! I'm not happy with that anymore. What happened to real Americans? You know – the "All Star" kind? The kind that fought and won World War II? The John Wayne or Ronald Reagan types? Where are those kinds of Americans today?

Do you think John Wayne would have settled for a stupid cheeseburger? No way! He would have jumped out of that minivan, wrestled a steer to the ground and I'd be snacking on a T-Bone faster than you could blink! Okay, maybe that's a stretch – but the question remains - why are we so complacent and spineless in this country?

As I touched on in Chapter 1, we're all to blame. Simply talking about it at the water cooler and then giving things a pass does nothing! Yet we all do it. We all whine about our little causes and issues and still we just take whatever Uncle Sam shoves down our throats next.

That's no way to be. It's not what this country and it's people are about. The U.S. Constitution didn't just write itself. That document exists (and is the hope of the world) because some great and brave folks took action – real action – and got the job done!

When John F. Kennedy said we were going to go to the moon, it got done because a great deal of people saw it as a worthy goal, got behind it and found a way to do it. Same as the personal and national sacrifices that went into the war efforts during World War II. A call went out, people recognized what needed to be done and they got busy – period.

Look at us now. We're all about text-messaging and Facebook and every little fringe "cause" you can imagine. But we have no "common thread" about us. Nearly three hundred million individual little countries, little tiny "Americas" running around. Each of them wanting what they consider as "theirs" and looking out for their own special "rights" and interests with no regard whatsoever for their fellow Americans and our common country as a whole.

Folks, we're missing the boat here!

Sure, we all enjoy our little past times and pursuing our own interests – we're supposed to do that. In a way, the Constitution encourages that sort of thing. That's why you have freedoms and rights so that you can live your life in the manner that you see fit. No problem there...

The problem is this self righteous kind of "entitlement fog" that so many of us walk around in. I'm not talking about Welfare or Social Security entitlement or anything as mundane as that – I'm referring to a well scripted attitude that most of us have.

You know, the:

"I'm busy doing my thing and somebody else needs to go and fix some problem that I like to gripe about but I won't lift a finger to look into it."

It's as though we're "free" to gripe, but that we're uniquely "entitled" to expect someone else to fix things.

That's crazy, that's self imposed apathy, and it's not working.

Now, go and multiply that attitude by a few hundred million and you begin to get an idea of the scale and scope of our common problem. It's not good.

Expecting things to work, to be fixed by others, while demanding your freedoms and liberties but not being willing to do your part is absolutely un-American.

Let me give you something to chew on. Consider this – Who's the better American in this example?

A man who owns a large business firm in a large U.S. city, who pays taxes and is griping to his associates about the "morons" in Washington <OR> a teenage girl floating on a home made raft from Cuba trying and praying to get into this country alive?

You may have guessed just from my wild scenario that I'm going to say "Cuban Girl". Know what? You'd be right.

This Cuban citizen is a better American because, at the end of the day, she's willing to sacrifice or even die for freedom and liberty, but most importantly, she's doing something about it.

There's no complacency in her actions, no apathy in her thoughts. In her mind, while she may not even call herself an "American", she's acting like a good one – and honestly – I pray she makes it here and finds all of her dreams! (I just hope we can deliver our part of the bargain.....)

You see, America, the physical country, is about boundaries and borders. It's just a geographic area on a map. On the other hand, Americans, the people, are everywhere! They live in countries that you can't even spell. They speak all sorts of languages and have all sorts of religions. They've never been here. Odds are they'll never get the chance to come here. But they are true Americans all the same.

Despite what you may think concerning "what the *world* thinks of America" - I personally don't buy into any of it - if it's negative.

The truth is – the world loves this country. They pray for and are envious of the things that we take for granted every day. They long for a place to freely vote. A place they can freely speak their mind. A place where they know that they can take their God given abilities and, if they could just be in a free enterprise market within a fair society, they could feed and clothe their families and grow to their potential.

In short – those that are depressed by tyranny pray to be in your shoes and would give their lives to trade with you.

This book, as a guide for the modern patriot would be useless without a close look at *us* as mutual benefactors and required defenders of liberty. It is our charge and duty as Americans' to vanguard freedom and be aware of any scenario where these liberties are encroached upon. Either abroad or at home. We owe it to our fellow Americans, no matter where they are in this world, to fight for liberty and freedom every day!.

Americans are supposed to be lovers of life and liberty. We celebrate freedom every July 4th. We can vote, we can carry a gun, we can speak our minds... and we are spoiled rotten. We are a mockery unto ourselves.

We wave our flag and our sparklers as we grill out, drink beer and then we bellyache about Washington and those who run the government. We have lost full sight of the fact that we run the government and have ourselves to blame for giving politicians the keys while they rob the store blind!

For far too long we have allowed *"crappy and consistent"* to creep into almost every aspect of our society and it has to stop! We go on at length whining about our government and politicians – stop it! We've had that done for us already! The Declaration of Independence covered that nicely. We have already been liberated from a government (Great Britain) that pushed itself to the point of tyranny and gave a deaf ear to the people. No more griping! Take action!

Bellyaching about the "government" in this country is like reinventing the wheel – it's already been done. The Constitution makes it clear that "We The People" are the one's in charge and the people of this country are not to create, deal with or support an oppressive, liberty strangling government. What we have today is the direct result of our own apathy – not a poorly designed Constitution or government!

All we need is to simply stop the tail from trying to wag the dog.

How do we do this? First we have to agree that *"crappy and consistent"* are no longer acceptable and then we have to join our efforts, just like our forefathers, and get focused on this as our one common goal.

"Crappy and consistent" is alive on both sides of the fence. Both in our government and in our people. Before we get to fixing our problems, we first have to recognize our problems.

I've included a few points to get it started. Each of these are issues where I see the idea of "crappy and consistent" living comfortably in our lives and our current apathetic thinking. I could write an entire book on these and honestly, I just pulled a few off the top of my head for inclusion here. But I'm sure that you have several of your own that you could include as well.

The overall point I'm trying to make, and I hope you consider this with your points too, is that you can see that "crappy and consistent is alive and well and hurting us. We need to end it.

CITIZENSHIP

Odds are, you were born here so you are a natural U.S. citizen. Lucky you.

But I hear a lot of people griping about illegals in this country. Mexicans who only sneak in here so that they can send money back home or others that may be here on extended Visas who just keep living off the "fat of the land". These people are "undeserving" and "taking things away from us!". "They don't deserve these things because they aren't citizens!"

Well, okay, time for a little humility. Let's find out if you're a true "American" or are you just coasting off of your birthright. It's time for a test. The same one that those who are striving for U.S. Citizenship have to take.

The following few pages contain 100 questions. These come from the question bank that those seeking their U.S. Citizenship have to study and take.

On test day they are asked 10 of these questions at random. They are required to correctly answer 6 out of 10 (only 60% is needed to pass.).

As someone who was born here and being exposed to American culture and history all of your life – you should fare far better than a lowly 60% - as a griping American you should hit 100%! Take the time and test yourself (answers are in the back of the book) and see how you do.

I'm sure that as a strong member of our society, able to gripe and ridicule, you will score nothing less than perfect. I know it's a slow way to start the book but don't skip this section. Stop what you're doing, get out a sheet of paper and pencil and start answering from memory. Good luck!

AMERICAN GOVERNMENT

A: Principles of American Democracy

1. What is the supreme law of the land?

2. What does the Constitution do?

3. The idea of self-government is in the first three words of the Constitution. What are these words?

4. What is an amendment?

5. What do we call the first ten amendments to the Constitution?

6. What is <u>one</u> right or freedom from the First Amendment

7. How many amendments does the Constitution have?

8. What did the Declaration of Independence do?

9. What are <u>two</u> rights in the Declaration of Independence?

10. What is freedom of religion?

11. What is the economic system in the United States?

12. What is the "rule of law"?

B: System of Government

13. Name <u>one</u> branch or part of the government.

14. What stops <u>one</u> branch of government from becoming too powerful?

15. Who is in charge of the executive branch?

16. Who makes federal laws?

17. What are the <u>two</u> parts of the U.S. Congress?

18. *How many U.S. Senators are there?*

19. We elect a U.S. Senator for how many years?

20. Who is <u>one</u> of your state's U.S. Senators now?

21. The House of Representatives has how many voting members?

22. We elect a U.S. Representative for how many years?

23. Name your U.S. Representative.

24. Who does a U.S. Senator represent?

25. Why do some states have more Representatives than other states?

26. We elect a President for how many years?

27. In what month do we vote for President?

28. What is the name of the President of the United States now?

29. What is the name of the Vice President of the United States now?

30. If the President can no longer serve, who becomes President?

31. If both the President and the Vice President can no longer serve, who becomes President?

32. Who is the Commander in Chief of the military?

33. *Who signs bills to become laws?*

34. Who vetoes bills?

35. What does the President's Cabinet do?

36. What are <u>two</u> Cabinet-level positions?

37. What does the judicial branch do?

38. What is the highest court in the United States?

39. How many justices are on the Supreme Court?

40. Who is the Chief Justice of the United States now?

41. Under our Constitution, some powers belong to the federal government. What is <u>one</u> power of the federal government?

42. Under our Constitution, some powers belong to the states. What is <u>one</u> power of the states?

43. Who is the Governor of your state now?

44. What is the capital of your state?

45. What are the <u>two</u> major political parties in the United States?

46. What is the political party of the President now?

47. What is the name of the Speaker of the House of Representatives now?

C: Rights and Responsibilities

48. There are four amendments to the Constitution about who can vote. Describe <u>one</u> of them.

49. What is <u>one</u> responsibility that is only for United States citizens?

50. Name <u>one</u> right only for United States citizens.

51. What are <u>two</u> rights of everyone living in the United States?

52. What do we show loyalty to when we say the Pledge of Allegiance?

53. What is <u>one</u> promise you make when you become a United States citizen?

54. How old do citizens have to be to vote for President?

55. What are <u>two</u> ways that Americans can participate in their democracy?

56. When is the last day you can send in federal income tax forms?

57. When must all men register for the Selective Service?

AMERICAN HISTORY

A: Colonial Period and Independence

58. What is <u>one</u> reason colonists came to America?

59. Who lived in America before the Europeans arrived?

60. What group of people was taken to America and sold as slaves?

61. Why did the colonists fight the British?

62. Who wrote the Declaration of Independence?

63. When was the Declaration of Independence adopted?

64. There were 13 original states. Name <u>three</u>.

65. What happened at the Constitutional Convention?

66. When was the Constitution written?

67. The Federalist Papers supported the passage of the U.S. Constitution. Name <u>one</u> of the writers.

68. What is <u>one</u> thing Benjamin Franklin is famous for?

69. Who is the "Father of Our Country"?

70. Who was the first President?

B: 1800s

71. What territory did the United States buy from France in 1803?

72. Name <u>one</u> war fought by the United States in the 1800s.

73. Name the U.S. war between the North and the South.

74. Name <u>one</u> problem that led to the Civil War.

75. What was <u>one</u> important thing that Abraham Lincoln did?

76. What did the Emancipation Proclamation do?

77. What did Susan B. Anthony do?

C: Recent American History and Other Important Historical Information

78. Name <u>one</u> war fought by the United States in the 1900s.

79. Who was President during World War I?

80. Who was President during the Great Depression and World War II?

81. Who did the United States fight in World War II?

82. Before he was President, Eisenhower was a general. What war was he in?

83. During the Cold War, what was the main concern of the United States?

84. What movement tried to end racial discrimination?

85. What did Martin Luther King, Jr. do?

86. What major event happened on September 11, 2001, in the United States?

87. Name <u>one</u> American Indian tribe in the United States.

INTEGRATED CIVICS

A: Geography

88. Name <u>one</u> of the two longest rivers in the United States.

89. What ocean is on the West Coast of the United States?

90. What ocean is on the East Coast of the United States?

91. Name <u>one</u> U.S. territory.

92. Name <u>one</u> state that borders Canada.

93. Name <u>one</u> state that borders Mexico.

94. What is the capital of the United States?

95. Where is the Statue of Liberty?

B: Symbols

96. Why does the flag have 13 stripes?

97. Why does the flag have 50 stars?

98. What is the name of the national anthem?

C: Holidays

99. When do we celebrate Independence Day?

100. Name <u>two</u> national U.S. holidays.

Check your answers and score yourself. (As I said, the answers are in the back of this book.) Your score is the number correct out of 100.

How did you do? I hope you did extraordinarily well. Meaning, I hope you did as well as the girl from Cuba would have tried for. I hope you didn't do like the man at the law firm and either score poorly or just pass it off as "fluff" or take the attitude that, "I'll come back later to that silly test part......".

No, I hope you took the time to stop what you were doing, actually take the test and then grade yourself.

Because what comes next will open your eyes *only* if you took the test.

Would you like to know my score? I scored an 86. Quite respectable but falling far short of where it should be. My score, and yours too, should have been perfect. I'll share part of my test experience (and my personal apathy) with you.

Take a look at question #64:

64) There were 13 original states. Name <u>three</u>.

I named 3 of them, and got it right – but not from having practiced knowledge of it. I remembered that the colonists established the eastern coast of the U.S. first. I gave it a little consideration and wrote down three *likely* states for my answer. I "felt" like I was right – but I wasn't 100% sure until I checked my answers.

Not the kind of mindset I should really have as an American. I should know all 13 of them, perfectly.

I'm not suggesting for one minute that we each get up in the morning, sing the National Anthem and recite the preamble to the Constitution. But it's a sad statement when I have to admit that I had to "guess" about the original states. When I was younger, in school and we studied American History, I could just rifle those 13 states right out of my mouth. No problem.

But it's a problem now.

You see, other things have taken priority in my mind. I've got bills, people to call back, my kids, all kinds of things going on in my life. But I also like to gripe whenever Capitol Hill does something stupid. I just shake my head and mutter under my breath. Trying to have my cake and eat it too.

What am I doing? I (along with you) have control over the outcomes in this country. But over time, like my prior American History knowledge, it's gotten eroded. Eroded with apathy and being distracted by other things. *"Crappy and consistent"*...

THIS IS WHAT WE HAVE TO RECOGNIZE AND ADDRESS AS A PEOPLE!

It's human nature. I'm just busy. I should expect my elected representatives to do what I think is best. After all, isn't that why we each pick the candidates that we do? Because we feel that they are like minded with us and would act as we would were we in their shoes.

Well, we *should* expect that.

However, we tend to let them run away with the store while we have our head down taking care of our own personal matters. Kind of a "set it and forget it" mentality – like a clock. Sadly, the busier and more complacent we are in our diligence concerning government – the better chances are that they can just do their little craft work and power grabs. As citizens, who Constitutionally run the government, we need to be very aware of politicians, their intentions and their actions.

This is where a renewed sense of Citizenship comes into play. I suggest that we work on this as a priority. It's important. Know your business about your country!

Oh, and if you didn't score 100% - well.... you think about it.

Be a Good Neighbor

I saw this online – can't remember where – but I wanted to share it with you.

A Recipe for a Good American
1/2 tablespoon honesty
1/2 tablespoon responsibility
1/2 tablespoon courage
1/2 tablespoon caring
1/2 tablespoon loyalty
1/2 tablespoon patriotism
1/2 tablespoon respect for
    the rights of others
1/2 tablespoon fairness

—Amanda Wittrup of Albuquerque, N.M.

This dear lady has it right. This is what it takes. The only thing I would change is to add a dash of "moral decency" until it tastes just right.

We, as a people, lack these consistent qualities and we pay the price for that everyday by being browbeaten and circumvented by our own Uncle Sam. We are consistent and crappy as fellow citizens toward each other.

A giant (and I mean GIANT) example of this is our welfare state in this country. There was a time, before most any of us remember, when there was no welfare system in this country. Do you know what people did in those days? What *true* Americans did?

They were good neighbors.

When someone in their community hit a streak of bad luck other people in that community came to the rescue. And no, it wasn't charity – it was true compassion and caring (see recipe above) and paying forward – because one never knew when they might need some help from their neighbors as well. It built stronger communities, it generated a sense of well being and good faith amongst people and ultimately, it's the right thing to do as a fellow human being.

But the Government Welfare system in this country is a train wreck. First of all, it creates a false sense of entitlement. If someone is down on their luck (or simply chooses to be) they expect a government check to come into their mailbox. Money sent to them from the sweat of the brows from people they have never met. Not their neighbors, not their friends – just numbers (low ones at that) on a piece of paper coming to their door.

I can assume in many instances that someone living in Chicago who is down on their luck certainly needs help. But so do the folks living in my community. I should be helping them, one on one – truly addressing their needs, while the good people of Chicago help to take care of their neighbors.

Constitutionally – Government run welfare makes no sense as it is not provided for within the Constitution. People were lovingly caring for each other long before the Constitution or even this country was formed. This fellowship and caring was practiced by our founders and they assumed that the good of mankind would continue this tradition of love.

The Welfare system clearly runs in this country as a mechanism to keep the downtrodden just that – downtrodden. Any modifications, entitlements and enhancements to the system are merely there to generate votes and to maintain a constituency of helpless, dependent voters.

Not good.

The damning effect of this is multifaceted – but the net effect is one of alienation for recipients and insulation for the taxpayer.

The recipient getting the money views it as "government money" - there's no such thing. Welfare money is the peoples' money being used to give the recipient support (and buy loyalty and enslavement by politicians) in the form of a check. The recipient can enjoy the luxury of insulation from that fact because the check is labeled "U.S. GOVERNMENT" and it comes from the "Welfare Department".

Taxpayers are insulated from active social (personal) involvement because the "Government" will take care of someone in need and there is no real reason for them to get involved. Our taxation pays for our apathy. (*Remember our "Entitlement Fog" on page 34?*) This allows the rest of us the luxury of getting on about our other business. After all, let Uncle Sam take care of the needy... that's what we pay taxes for... right?

The ultimate loser in this scheme? All of us – all the citizens – welfare recipients or not. We are now, thanks to a welfare system, alienated from each other. And because of the taxing scheme, we are divided into "classes". Face it, we're either on Welfare or we aren't. Thanks to Uncle Sam, we don't really have to help each other or look out for each other.

Who then is receiving benefit from this system? No one but the politicians. The whole mess centers around induced propaganda, induced need and induced guilt from our own government in opposition of our good will and nature.

After all, you're an American right? Aren't Americans benevolent? Aren't we always willing to help our neighbor? Sure we are. So, let's all pull together (through taxes) and feed a welfare system that will help those of us who are enduring bad times.

At first blush – this seem very rational and logical. Problem is, it doesn't work.

This country was not founded on those principles. The idea is for you to have the freedom of choice to do with your money and property as you wish. If you choose to help those in need with whatever blessings you can share – more power to you and thank you for being an outstandingly fine American.

However, if you choose not to help someone, that is also your choice and you have every right not to participate in that effort. It is your right to choose and, that's American as well.

By removing the rights of the people to not be able to choose we lose the ability to control how the money is spent and this causes animosity and a rip in our social fabric as well as empowering those that give the money away the luxury and ability to fish for votes with it.

Negative and and obvious examples of this failing system are many. One, is simply watching people abuse the system – literally making a career out of working the paperwork and drawing several checks as they pose as several different (sometimes imaginary or deceased) recipients. Another, and far worse is knowing that it's a downward spiral and seeing it have a negative impact on the individual recipient. In other words, they become addicted and dependent on welfare – wallowing in an endless cycle of self and government inflicted poverty.

This literally strips that individual of liberty. They "miss out" on the American Dream. The chance to have hope and develop and grow the want and passion for something more than what they have and who and what they are. That's a "double dipping" effect and it pains those of us who wish they could see what's happening to them and would take the initiative to break this terrible cycle. They could tend to blame their station in life on unrealistic or non pending factors. Blaming the wealthy or big business when all the while it's the bigger nanny state force feeding them and keeping them acclimated to an eternal state of dependency (all in the name of gaining their vote).

I probably rambled on a little long there, but I really wanted to make a solid point. The government is not our nanny – it is our servant – but politicians have managed to dissect the psyche of the public and use the best parts of us against us in the name of good will. (You may not have studied a candidate before you voted for them, but rest assured, they have thoroughly studied you!) I wanted to dismantle and define the welfare system's effects within the scope of the American (and decent) way of looking out for our neighbors.

This is important to recognize because, if you'll look around you a bit, you'll begin to see that a vast majority of things like these are rooted in the twisting of politicians and played up or against the good nature of the American people. A wolf in sheep's clothes so to speak.

For instance, we can run the math on this a million times and prove that it's a no win. We can readily point out that the welfare system is a vote buying machine and a tool of enslavement for those down on their luck. We can talk about good American spirit, charity, benevolence... you name – but it gets cast aside whenever a politician speaks up in opposition to your good reasoning.

They'll tell you that you simply have no sympathy for those poor souls. They'll say that you are too rich or fortunate to understand the true hardships that these people have. That only the government can mobilize help on this scale to feed them. To clothe them. To educate them. To doctor them... the list goes on.

Bull!

I want to see us take back the reigns and be in control of our own good characteristics and our love for our fellow man. I don't want to see the brainwashing continue in our young where we teach them to love their neighbor, help provide for them in time of need – only to have them be told by others and begin to believe that by pooling all of the peoples efforts (money) together, the Government can take better care of the unfortunate than their own neighbors or local community. It's just not true.

Every answer to all of our problems can't be done with the wave of a Government magic wand. We desperately need to get our citizenship skills polished up, realize that the government isn't going to help or subsidize it without a voter being pandered to and take back this important power that we all have within our own hearts and good nature.

If we do this, without fail and without flinching, the need for Uncle Sam to "come to the rescue" will soon go away – and so will the politicians' reach and power.

Be a GREAT American!

I want each of us to agree upon and act on the following:

Today, I will find some way to help someone who needs help.

That's it. Simple really. I don't mean throw some change in a bucket to help someone get some sort of surgery (although you can do that too), I mean *help* someone. Go grocery shopping for someone who is sick and housebound. Help raise some money for a church. Go cut the grass at the volunteer fire station.... whatever. Find a way to help. Don't let need come looking for you! You go and find the need and fulfill it. If you alone can't help, call in more help.

That's the power of "We the People". There's no limit as to how much help and effort we can generate. The "government" is of only finite size, resources and money. Not us! And that's the point to doing this. It will give you a front row seat as to how much you really can do and how much we as a people can do when we combine together!

The people can provide two things that Uncle Sam can NEVER do.

One is the money. The people of this country have an unlimited supply of money (Which is why Uncle Sam is constantly trying to get more of it!). Plus, there is no end to our ingenuity in making the stuff (money). We have a workforce and brain-trust larger than any on the entire planet.

Don't tell me of the countries that have more "citizens", hence more workforce. Fact is, we're the best there is. We were raised in a free market system and simply put – American citizens are (when left to our own devices and without the government noodling in it) genius at business, business growth and production. Period.

The second is care and compassion. Ever been in line at the DMV or any other line where you had to interface with government?

Now by golly that is some fine – fine – fine customer service...... (clearly I'm joking).

And that's just it. If you are dependent upon the government for anything – then you need to realize that they don't care about you! There's no love there like a neighbor or a friend can provide.

When you're in a Government line, you're not a citizen who pays their salary – you're a customer. Get over it. If you are on Welfare – you're a customer. Social Security? Customer. WIC? Customer. Pick any program you like... Customer.

Plus, you're the best kind of customer. You're a "captive" customer.

As a people, we didn't go shopping to find the best deal on our Welfare, Social Security, Medicaid or Medicare. You are a captive to the only game in town and the keepers of those reigns DON'T CARE ABOUT YOU! Truth is, while it's illegal for you and I to operate like this in a business sense, the Government can and gets to run a monopoly.

I want you to see that you, me and all of us are the best. The best at taking care of ourselves and our neighbors, looking out for the general welfare of all things in this country and that we are the absolute masters of being in charge of our own lives and destinies. Don't believe me? Read the Constitution.

Be a great American by being the best in the world. It's what we're all about. Think of that recipe I showed you! Live those things in your home and help those around you do the same.

Let's focus on honesty, responsibility, courage, caring, loyalty, patriotism, respect for the rights of others, fairness and morality. THESE are the things that only we can provide and produce, not the Government, only AMERICANS can do that. Me, you, our neighbors. Grandstand and stump all they want, make campaign promises, bicker in the House and Senate – but politicians cannot make this happen.

This is what we have to offer that scares politicians to death.

They don't want us looking out for each other and caring – that's *their* self appointed job. Using tax money turned into social program money as "vote bait" and increasing their stronghold on our day to day lives. It's a farce. They simply cannot have any love for you more than their love of your vote.

A voting customer at their monopoly store.

When we love our fellow American and come to his aid, when we act honestly and compassionately, when we have decency, moral character, and share those qualities with others - we are in charge. That's when we are running the country. Being all of those things and watching over the government, controlling it with our votes and voices is the only time we are truly being great Americans.

Strengthen our Families

We've gotten pretty "crappy and consistent" in this department over the past generation or so. Sure, we love our children and we value the times we all spend together – but they are few and far between. Busy, busy, busy with Soccer and Little League, Ladies Night Out, Poker Night for the boys... this list goes on.

We need to spend some continual quality time together and re-bond as families – not just exist as families. Get involved with each others lives, develop some real cares for each and let them know that going fishing together as a family is just as important as your Poker Night.

This future of this country is dependent on our young growing up with great core values. There's no better place to learn compassion and good citizenship than at home.

These are only a few examples, but I think that you can see a consistent thread. In short, reacquaint yourself with your good nature, stand up for it and be behind it – backing it all the way. Settle for nothing less than excellence in every corner of your life.

Crappy and consistent can get a job done – but it can never provide the level of excellence that we Americans should demand, deliver and expect at every turn. From our jobs, our personal prideful performance at those jobs, in our communities and in the care and compassion for our friends and neighbors.

There are a million little things that can define what an American is – but from now on, there can only be one type that will see us through... Great Americans.

Starting today, being an American can no longer mean just taking what's laid before us. We can no longer be passive in our thinking or in the protection of our liberties and freedoms.

Being an American has to be more than being apathetic. It also has to be more than holding our heads high, wrapping a flag around us and riding off on our Harley Davidson's thinking of fireworks, BBQ and beer. Romantic... but not very effective.

I want a country where excellence is once again the norm. Where being the best and taking the steps to be the best are forefront in our mind. I want a Government that trembles whenever our feet shuffle because they know that we are united and that we are the most powerful voice representing freedom, liberty, human rights and fairness in the world.

That's what I want, it's what you should want and only we, Great Americans, can do that.

CHAPTER

3

Divided We Fall

Being a "Great American" is so important if we are ever going to regain the proper order of things in this country. "Divided We Fall" was designed to be brief, but I could write an entire book on the roles and importance of that American spirit.

Having said that – this will be a tough chapter to keep short. So, as "briefly" as I can I want to try and explain to you how politicians "work" the system and how it's used against us.

Believe me, brevity here will be a struggle.

The main thing I want you to notice in this chapter is that politicians love smoke and mirrors, power and their elitism over you. Sadly they do this by using our laws, rules, good feelings, emotions and intent against us. Watch for these in this chapter (and in our daily lives).

Division Amongst the People

What if we had a country where there was no religious strife, no racial barriers, no toes being stepped on, less crime and violence, the country was solvent (no national debt), people have their liberties and freedoms and everything went smoothly. Isn't that a great dream and goal?

Not if you're a politician.

That's the politicians worst nightmare. How are they going to run a campaign where they try to defend you, your rights, your business, your money and your special interest if these so called "problems" went away? How could they feel your *pain* if you had none?

Think about it. It's not really a stretch of the imagination at all. Truth is, they don't want these things to get fixed. They need our little gripes and strife's so that they can swoop in to the rescue and be your little rock star hero!

Politicians revel in our woes and sorrows. It's what keeps them in business. From a Constitutional standpoint, the Federal Government is only supposed to defend the country on a national scale, move the mail and make federal law. Period. Politicians aren't supposed to be our collective earthly savior. The Constitution clearly points out that the people are in charge and that the Federal Government needs to keep it's nose out of peoples business.

In order to keep us "punch drunk", off balance and to keep the pot stirred, they pass any "socially stupid" law they can dream up. This puts turmoil on "auto pilot". Once we're pandered to and some particular "voice" gets a law passed for them or their issue, it starts a quiet firestorm in the public who must simply swallow it.

A great example of one of these things are our "hate crime laws". If you hate someone because of race or ethnicity and kill them, there hasn't been just a murder – there's been a "hate crime". Now, unfortunately the real crime is the same – someone is dead.

And that's just the point – someone is dead! It doesn't matter what the motive was – someone... is... DEAD!

But now, thanks to our all knowing and all feeling politicians, we can get additional penalties on our freedoms like more gun controls or some other clamp on your liberties to try and stop this murderous "racial madness"!

Big Brother will try to score additional ground here because, clearly, passing "hate crime" laws will not thwart or stop interracial crime. (because nothing ever will, as long as we have more than one race in this country) So, off they go to write more freedom bending laws, tighten their grip, and we have to deal with the sad reality of a death that's being capitalized on by politicians. The pot stays stirred.

This is ludicrous.

Politicians are little drama queens. I saw a television show the other night where a woman asked a man - "Do you love me?" He answered, "Yes......" Her eyes welled up with tears and she darted off saying, "I don't even know why you try..........."

What in the world was that? I asked myself. Heaven help the poor fool if he had said "no". The main thing is, the fella answered sincerely and accurately – but it was clear that no matter which way he answered – he was toast. Same principle in action with our politicians. They speak out of both sides of their mouth without ever lending us an ear. No matter which way we try and move, we're pretty much damned if we do and damned if we don't.

In the same notion as our little "hate crime" example, we also have this little gem called "reverse discrimination". Now this is how I understand it – well, I don't *understand* it, but here is what I "think" I understand about it.

A white person acts racist or biased against a black person (or any other racial group) – that's called discrimination. But if a black person (or any other racial group) does the same to a white person, that's a case of "reverse" discrimination.

This just totally eludes me, my thinking and my intelligence. If black against white discrimination is "reverse discrimination" should white against black discriminating be called "normal discrimination"? How about "forward discrimination"? Again it's just ludicrous.

Discrimination is discrimination. It's against the law. One law. One single law. We don't need a "special term" and some other "special law" for the <u>exact</u> <u>same</u> <u>thing</u>!

We're so gullible and stupid! Things like this exists because politicians need us all to be rough around the edges and have social sore spots with each other. Remember, the last thing a politician can ever allow is for the citizens of this country to solve their problems without them. And truth is, we're going to have to start solving these problems on our own because politicians will never allow themselves to be voluntarily removed from the equation! It's like some psycho mother from the movies that won't let their children grow up and leave the house because they "need her!". That's just wrong.

This is the fox watching the hen house. Politicians clamor for and pass "special laws" for "special things" reminding us that we need them in order to stay together as a society. All the while we never realize that they are the ones intentionally creating divides and rifts that they can politicize and polarize the people over.

Realize who you are and your part in their plans.

The perfect American citizen (voter), to a politician, is somehow connected to a large group that can *also* be categorized as a minority. I don't mean a racial minority – that's too easy.

That minority could be Union members. It could be middle class business owners. It could be people wanting to save the environment.... you name it. To keep their leverage and power alive - their goal is to have us <u>all</u> belonging to some sort of special interest group (minority).

Minorities of any kind, are perfect targets for a candidate looking for votes. You see, a vote is power. And they (during their campaigns) attempt to work that power out of your hand through your own individual weaknesses and social issues. They sell it to you as though, when you vote for "them", they'll make sure that *you* are heard in Washington!

I hate to break the bad news to you but that's pure folly. Just do the math. <u>No politician can ever get elected by trying to do the bidding of any minority</u>. A minority alone cannot mathematically bring enough votes to the table to ever win an election. So, while a politician can talk about their support of "Gay Portuguese immigrants who want to save the rain forests." until they turn blue, you can bet that they are also pandering to the Hispanics, Black Business managers, the Unions, Teachers and Housewives. It's a numbers game.

Lost your core? Prepare to get swindled!

If you voted for a candidate to help support your "cause" - or because they are going to help fight for you, your people or your special interests, you got swindled. You just gave your vote away to a con-man! (or con-woman.)

That's why there's so much talk these days on getting back to "core values". Special interests can be handled at the "people" level quite efficiently and effectively if we don't let politicians stir the pot and quit trying to buy votes with "favors" given to the public. As Americans, huddled together and working as one people we only have one message to continually re-vote back into any office... Liberty and Freedom.

Liberty and Freedom is our only, collective "special interest".

Politicians are scared to death of "core values" (the kind I talk about in this book) because they can't "work" or manipulate those issues – not from a Constitutional standpoint. There's no "spin" that they can put on it. That's why the Constitution is so important. All they can do is to try and paint those that care about their freedoms as "nut jobs".

Labeling those who love liberty as anything but a true American is a dangerous, dangerous tactic. It reeks of folks like Hitler and Stalin and no politician has the American right to do so.

I often, kiddingly, tell people on the phone, when they ask me what I'm doing, that I'm, "..just sitting here clinging to my Bible and polishing my gun....". It always gets a chuckle! But it's a good point.

In the 2008 Presidential campaign, the good folks of Pennsylvania were considered "backward" for "Clinging to their Guns and Religions". Sad. How in the world can a politician be considered for an office in this country when they chastise or ridicule two of the most basic rights guaranteed by the Constitution. It's a defilement of public trust and a real slap in the face of the citizens who choose to exercise those Constitutional rights – especially when so many people of the world are denied them.

Our core values and rights guaranteed under the Constitution should never be made light of by anyone – especially a politician of our own.

People, good people (and there are still a few left in Washington) are all about core values and not about stirring the pot. I don't want a law protecting me from "Reverse Discrimination" - I don't want anybody discriminating against anyone at all. Not because there's a law against it but because it goes against my core values. There's no need for strife and all of these "special interests" we all have. As a matter of fact, dropping those things is vital to solving our problems today – all of them!

The more we dial down our intellect, allow ourselves to be swindled and generally lose sight of what our "core values" are – the more we lose our liberties and freedoms to politicians.

Please don't let that happen!

Get your senses tuned up and get down to your core. When politicians start working both ends against the middle – they are simply tightening their grip on our throats. Don't let them. Take the advice from Chapter 2 and be a "Good American".

Get your heart off of your sleeve. You underestimate your fellow American and the size and scale of us and our greatness as a people.

If you are in a minority and feel like you're being slighted against – first check your attitude. Is it really happening? If it isn't, and be honest with yourself, drop it. If it is happening, tell someone. Share the experience and find a sympathetic ear. Don't go around screaming about it and making a fool of the issue. You may be pleasantly surprised that there are many, many great people (Americans) around you that will help you solve this.

I'm not trying to suggest that you give someone a pass for stepping on your toes – after all, you're an American and you deserve the same rights and liberties as anyone else. Not more... but certainly not less. I truly have a ton of faith in the American people – and I'm willing to bet that in most cases, great people will come to your aid.

Now, if it's a matter of life or death – literally, hit that PANIC button with a sledge hammer. If you are surrounded in a parking lot at night with a bunch of thugs wanting to do you harm – scream bloody murder and get help! But be aware, that most issues are very simple social ones (work discrimination for instance) and don't need to have CNN show up. The media just loves to twist things up and the politicians lay in the grass waiting to jump on a social problem with more legislation and leverage.

Whether it be a race issue, religion... anything – we've got to get out of the "Hit the PANIC button" mode that we seem to be in. That's an "out" created by the politicians. It gives them the "moral authority" to write some more laws and regulations that trim a little more of your liberties away. Be aware of the manipulation and the capitalization that politicians make out of your "issues". Truth is, your pain is their gain!

Again, pay attention to how this mechanism works and learn to smell and hear them when they try their tricks. They can't and won't take care of us like we can. Let them know that you're wise to their little shell game. Let them know that your vote is not "for sale". Let them know that you refuse to be swindled. Don't let them divide us.

If we're divided we'll fall like a bunch of blocks with no mortar.

Solid as we are, we can't be stacked effectively unless we can stick together. We can only do that through our "core values". They know that we have the spirit and integrity that they so desperately lack. Stick together everyone! Don't let them "work" us into separate little groups. We aren't! We are one people, depending on each other to stand strong. Like the Pledge of Allegiance says - "indivisible". Let's be that way! Indivisible!

They need us weak and dependent upon them so they can have a lever. Which makes the fact that they are so entrenched in everything we have and do just abhorrent! We've given them the keys to our lives. Get them back. Stand strong. Be unified and make them sweat.

Sure, we all have our differences and different concerns about the world around us. There's no way around it. White folks aren't black, Buddhists can't really grasp Christianity. Those difference are natural. But it doesn't mean that they MUST clash. All the laws that are imposed upon us concerning these things are, considered by politicians, necessary to keep the America people running smoothly. It's to minimize strife. Their thinking says, that if we have to compromise our liberties (i.e. the Constitution) for the benefit of the whole, then so be it.

No way.

The Constitution is already in place for the "whole" - everyone. It clearly states that we all have the same rights. There should be no government "bending" of the rules under the guise of helping the "whole". That's socialism. A politician always checks the Constitution last rather than first making sure that their "will" passes muster. After all, think of all they could do for us if that pesky Constitution wasn't in their way!

We're Americans, we can and will get through all of our interpersonal strife. We always have and we always will. There is no way in the world that minimizing our rights and freedoms (our liberties) as a people can ever be constructive.

Let's take it back!

Every time you help someone, you pause and consider someone besides yourself or their feelings on a subject, you are regaining a piece of America for Americans and away from the politicians. It takes, and is going to take, some effort. We're out of shape socially. Most of us sit around lifting nothing (with self imposed elitism or apathy) while those rare few are hoisting shovels trying to be good, decent citizens and Americans.

Stop it.

Those with the shovels, take a break. Everyone else, grab a spoon!

That's all it takes. Everyone doing just a little bit – just a drop.

Benjamin Franklin said, *"Many hands make light work"*. He's right.

Don't ever forget that and don't underestimate what value your tiny contribution will make. Consider what saying something as simple as, "Thank You" might mean to someone or holding a door open for them could do. Remember, we are excellent!

It's small, it's little and yes, it matters.

We're not the best in the world just because we say we are. Remember and think about all the people in this world who really do look up to us. Who would give anything to be as lucky as you are by just being an American and being on this soil.

We get all bent out of shape and feel let down when one of our sport or celebrity "hero's" does something stupid or they become too full of themselves - for being spoiled or arrogant. Now, take a look at yourself. A long serious look. Let's not be that kind of "hero".

Want to be the light of the world and ruin a politicians day? Be a Great American! Count your blessings, love liberty and your personal independence, look out for your neighbor and in short – spread the love!

Remember, our inner national peace and brotherhood is their worst political nightmare!

Smoke and Mirrors

Let's spend a little time looking at some of the more visible tricks that are used to further divide us as a people.

Some of these are subtle, some of these are obvious, but they are devices that are used by politicians constantly. Sad part is that they've been done for so long that they have weaved themselves into the fabric of our everyday culture in America. "It's always been that way." is the common response to old, bad habits. However, that can no longer be our excuse.

Get your head tuned up and start watching and looking for these things. The couple that I've included certainly aren't the only examples, but these are a few of the biggies I thought we should cover.

The main thing is to be realistic about the world around you. We are fooled every day by these "tricks" that have been hardened into law or habit. Become aware of them and, humbly, realize that we are being manipulated and used.

Gerrymandering

The term "gerrymandering" gets it's name from the politician Elbridge Gerry. Mr. Gerry was the governor of Massachusetts from 1810 to 1812. The term is a mash up of words between

the governor's last name, Gerry and the word "salamander".
(It's a little water lizard.)

"Gerrymander" first appeared in the Boston Gazette on March 26, 1812 which ran this image as an example.

Governor Gerry enacted a clever law that would allow his state to be redistricted in such a way as to benefit his own political party. In doing so, one of the new and contorted districts looked a great deal like a dragon. Playing on the mythic ideal of that beast and probably as well as the myth of the "logic" in justifying this new redistricting scheme, the term stuck.

Okay, what does this mean to you? Gerrymandering is when a politician has normally separate and divided districts (that they can gather support within) banded together making it almost impossible to <u>ever</u> vote them out of office.

This is dirty and dividing.

The negative impacts of this trick on the voter are plenty.

The biggest one is loss of voter power. Those that don't like this candidate and are voting against them within their gerrymandered district technically have a nullified vote. This is because you are outnumbered by connecting (although loosely) areas that strongly support the candidate. In short – you lose your true voting power.

Secondly, it creates an imbalanced representation of the people in the voice of government, which is not Constitutionally fair. In reality, the boundaries of districts should be evenly and geographically distributed. This allows all the people within any area an equal voice in voting and in matters concerning themselves and their government.

If a candidate gerrymanders an area so as to exclude those that won't vote for them, then they are only representing their choice of selected voters. The net result is that you have someone in office who is not representing a fair slice of the American public.

Let's say that you have 2 open seats in office waiting to be filled. One candidate is from a gerrymandered area that will always vote for them, the other candidate is being voted on from the other rag-tag group of "left-over" areas. Both candidates win within their respective districts – and both are from differing political parties. Both candidates also won their district in a landslide. Or did they?

Assume that the Gerrymandered candidate won 70% of his district, the other candidate won 90% of theirs. Still viable wins within a district – but if you were to redistribute the districts correctly and fairly you could see where the outcome may not have been the same. If those numbers were cut in half, say as a popular vote on an average, they could each have only 35% and 45% respectively. The 45% (non gerrymandered) candidate may very well still have won their district but the gerrymandered contender possibly wouldn't have.

At only 35% of the votes, that leaves ample room for a candidate from an opposing party to have won, thus sending two of the same party type candidates to their offices. This might reflect more realistically the true and even makeup of the voting people back home. Gerrymandering prevents this truth from coming to light. Insane.

This is merely a hypothetical on my part and a bending/playing of the numbers. However, I'm trying to bend those numbers *back* toward reality – not away from it as gerrymandering does. The larger issue is that, as long as gerrymandering is allowed, we'll never know the true numbers and who actually, fairly won. In short – the peoples wishes, as a whole, will not be represented. This is unfair and wrong and is a perfect example of government politicians dividing us for their career needs.

Are you suffering from Gerrymandering where you live? The best thing to do is to go online or to your library and look at the district maps that concern you. If it's in a nice little geometric grid, you're probably alright, but if it's broken up into odd chunks scattered about or runs along some strange lines, you may be in trouble. (Think of the diagram from earlier.)

Bottom line, this practice must end! It's just another way that we are diminished as a people and carved down into little groups that feed the specific need for the career politician.

Gerrymandering is clear evidence that you don't matter to politicians, unless your vote can help them get elected and further their stay in political office. Remember, as modern day Patriots we must demand equality and fairness for all people. Period. That means all of us being heard equally and all of us being equally represented. No more Gerrymandering!

Taxation, Tax Code, Income Tax, etc.

The U.S. Tax Code, the written rules, laws and regulations concerning Federal taxation in the United States is a behemoth. The code itself is nearly 70,000 pages (that's not a typo – Seventy THOUSAND pages). Give or take, it's actually closer to 66,000 almost 67,000 – but give it just a little more time, it'll be 70,000+ pages before you know it.

Let me give you an idea as to how much text that is. The book in your hands is what's known as a "digest" size book. About a third short of having the same text area of a regular size sheet of printer paper. This book has approximately 170 pages.

Multiply 67,000 (the tax code pages) times a third (to make up for our pages being a 1/3 short of a full sheet) and add that back to 67, 000

67,000 X .33333 = 22,333.331

$$
\begin{array}{r}
67,000 \\
+22,333.311 \\
\hline
89,333.311
\end{array}
$$

We'll just round that down to 89,333. What does this number represent? That's how many pages the tax code would take if it were printed in the size book you hold now.

Let's divide this by the 170 or so pages that this book contains.

89,333 / 170 = 525.4882353

That number, again rounded down is 525. That's the number of copies we would need of "Divided We Fall" to contain the current U.S. Tax Code. Want to have some more fun? This book is about 4/10th of an inch thick.

525 X 0.40(inches) = 210 Inches.

Divided by 12 inches (to give us an answer in feet) = 17.5

So, a stack of "Divided We Fall" just a smidge over 17 and a half feet tall, could contain the current U.S. Tax code. To give you an idea of scale, most of you are probably in a room that has 8 or 9 foot high ceilings. So, our books stacked floor to ceiling twice ought to just about cover it.

It doesn't take a rocket scientist (maybe it does) to figure that those pages contain a great deal more than figuring out what percentage you must pay the Government based on your total yearly income. As a matter of fact, under scrutiny, it's painfully obvious what it's for.

If the income tax system in this country were about simply collecting taxes (fairly with equal taxation and representation for all the citizens) then we would have a flat tax. A tax where everyone pays the same percentage.

But that's not what our income tax system of today is all about.

The tax code is filled (17 ½ feet high) with twisting and turnings so complex that no one can understand it in it's entirety. That twisting and turning is designed to help some people – while penalizing others.

Do you have a large corporation that might need to try and save a little on taxes or are some special interest group that needs a break? Well, the proper campaign contribution can probably help bury a few new lines of special code in the document made just for you.

~Or~

You could be making politicians look bad or be public enemy #1 and here come the audits. (Think Al Capone, Martin Luther King Jr. or any Wall Street Executive getting a bonus).

I ask you – in a land of liberty and equality how is this fair or even possible?

This is why the politicians made such an issue over big bonuses recently given to executives on Wall Street. They have to be demonized (because big business is the source of all evil in this country... not the politicians – *remember*??) over all that money they are making.

I want you to think about this very seriously for a moment, and to some folks reading this, I know I'm preaching to the choir, but I'd like everyone to follow along closely.

The bonuses in question are clouded and shrouded in political finger pointing and ethical twists. These bonuses were paid to people who worked for or were contracted to corporations that received Federal Bailout money.

But I ask you, was it ethical for the Government to demand the bonus money back or not? Was it legal for the Government to tax (retroactively mind you) nearly 90% of it?

That's not equal taxation with representation. That's using the authority of the IRS and the Federal Income Tax to clearly target and penalize specific individuals. While it's wrong under any circumstances and taxation as manipulation has always gone on, this was done blatantly, out in the open and visible to all.

The Federal Government did nothing short of financially putting the cross-hairs on someone and then pulled the trigger.

President Obama likes to use the term, "teachable moment". I'll borrow that and use it here myself.

This was a teachable moment for sure. We (Americans) had a moment here to stand up for what was right and we failed. We saw them fire a proverbial shot at people who had done nothing wrong and we gave it a pass. We were too caught up in the "financial and economic" moment and our special interest, to call foul! We watched the Government single out individuals (not a company mind you – individual employees) and witnessed them using taxation as a weapon. Had these people broken a business law or any other law by taking their bonuses that would have been a different story. But they didn't.

Whether you like it or not, those people received the money that they were contractually entitled to and we let the government, through a twisting of power and authority deny these people of what was rightfully their property and steal it from them. We let the politicians extend their reach, make a power play, include it into the Tax Code (law) and that over reaching authority, through precedence will remain.

Do you grasp that? It will remain. Waiting to grab you and your income if they feel that the need arises. Not based on common sense, ethics or legality. (Although we've let them make it legal now...) They are ready to take your personal property and money, at the individual level, with no wrong doing of your own, if they so desire. This was wrong. Legally, morally and spiritually wrong.

And we let them do it. Our apathy has given them this power. The shame on each of us should be worn like a scarlet letter.

There's more to this "teachable moment". Do you understand the word precedence? Precedence is an original event that sets a standard. Now, thanks in large part to our apathy, it can be a standard procedure to single out an individual for making money and just take it from them on the reasons of politically defined principles. Not law or even in fairness. Just because.

As is the case with the entire Tax Code. Pages upon pages of exceptions for some and penalties for others. This is absolutely unconstitutional and un-American.

As far as constitutionality, equality under the law or even morality, answer this question for me:

Are people who pay more taxes entitled to more representation in the house and senate than those who don't pay any taxes or pay few taxes?

They should be. Since we stand for the ideal of "No taxation without representation". Those that pay more taxes should get more representation – right? They don't. Big business and the wealthy are always under fire where the taxation and government are concerned. If anything, the largest recipient of social monies in this country go to those that do not make an income nor pay income taxes at all. This is totally backwards – and – with proper thought – totally unconstitutional.

The real danger here is the trickle down effect. As those that earn the most make less money from their businesses being squeezed, they slip into a lower income taxing bracket. In order to maintain the tax money inflow to the coffers the taxation brackets must slide down with them forcing higher percentages collected on less money made. In short, each year the dollar definition of what constitutes "wealthy" must drop. (Originally, Income Tax was imposed on only the top 1% of wage earners.)

Pretty soon, that number will have to bottom out and it will ultimately run smack into the top of the poverty level. Meaning that everyone will be taxed, selectively if need be, in order to feed the "machine". Couple that with a huge growing deficit and out of control spending and you can see where the concept of taxing at 90+% on anyone getting any bonus begins to be a possibility.

Conspiracy theory? Black helicopters? Big Brother?

Nope, simple math. Look at the situation and run the numbers through your own head.

I also hear many people go on about the Constitutionality of the 16th (XVI) amendment (Income Tax Amendment) and whether or not it's constitutional. Entire books have been written on this subject and there is quite a movement of people who follow this idea. Don't play with this fire!

Whether your argument about it is valid or not, there are many good people sitting in Federal Prison who went up against this thing and failed in the courts. Fair or not, it's now in there. (It's a part of the Constitution once amended.) Fighting against an Amendment is stupid idea. Working to have it abolished is another.

This country needs either a flat income tax or a national sales tax (fair tax) to stop this foolishness. It's the absolute best thing. This is where you pay a flat percentage of your income no matter if you make $1000 a year or in the Billions. Simple, elegant, collects plenty of money and the best part? Gives you back a great deal of your liberty and freedom.

You see, if the government were to make just 10% to 20% of every dollar made (or spent) in this country there would be money flowing everywhere. Plus two GREAT benefits.

1) People wouldn't try and dodge the tax laws or have to scrounge around for receipts to prove their deductions because it's too easy and traceable. You make $500 a week. Uncle Sam gets $50. Easy.

2) Government would help businesses grow and really assist people needing jobs. This time for real! Because if the Fed's know that they are in for a true cut and it's the only way they can collect taxes – it makes perfect sense to get some of the laws and restriction out of the way of business. They would want you to get a raise and to have all your friends go to work. The more people in the work force, making more and more money, the more taxes that are collected.

As much sense as this makes, politicians (those currently in office) will fight tooth and nail against it! You may ask yourself, why would they have opposition against a simpler system that would work and generate more tax income? Because they don't want it simple. You can't hide favors or inflict penalties or imprisonment by using a simple and fair system. They would lose their leverage and power!

Politicians need the Tax Code. They need it to overtax the rich, justifying it with vilification. They need an "average" tax amount out there so that they can buy votes by allowing certain voters "tax breaks" and they also need a system so that if an individual gets "out of line" they can be beaten back into submission with threat of penalty or prison. It's another way to divide and conquer us, keep us unbalanced through unfair taxation and representation and it's a power that they won't readily let go of.

In these short and select examples, it's easy to see that so much of bureaucracy today hinges on the idea of complexity and division. The Government is a giant, giant machine and is very complex. This is like the Space Shuttle. It's a cool thing – but its specialization and complexity make it super expensive to operate and maintain. Complex systems require specialized care in order to keep them running and makes both of them prone to breakdown, damage and disaster. However, given the mission of a spacecraft, you can understand the necessity of some level of complexity. This machine is required to travel through hostile conditions and operate in a very extreme environment.

Not the U.S. Government.

It's operation is overly complex by want of those who currently operate it. It's mission is also intentionally complicated. It can be done much simpler.

Once people finally realize that the only Constitutional purpose and role of Government is to manage affairs for the country and combine the States, a gigantic number of problems will immediately go away. But as long as politicians use that government as a platform for power and the elongation of a career, we will have giant, massive, overly complicated problems.

It's time to recognize all the ways that politicians work so hard to maintain their power and divide us. Any time the government and the politicians are allowed to discriminate against us, to look upon us all as minorities instead of people and manipulate or demonize us based on our status – we are losing....

Losing our self worth, losing our importance as human beings and, most importantly, our role in government as "the boss".

Never let them divided us. Ever. Because divided, we fall.

CHAPTER

4

Liberty and Justice for All

While it's true that we've made our own mess and the simple answer could be a national chorus of, "Vote the bums out!", it's just not that easy.

We've all heard the term, "Grass roots effort" - and yes, it's going to take that kind of spirit to get this fixed, there's more to it than that. We could sit here and lament at length over which politician or group did what, or go on and on about what's wrong in D.C. (and honestly, there's a time for that), but we need to do some "social" housekeeping first.

I've already suggested that it's the differences between us, our special interests, that politicians use to either divide us or manipulate us with. That's an obvious trick. But let's not totally disregard that it's also one of our biggest strengths. You see, diversity is a powerful thing. We don't need to become some homogenous group of robots all believing the exact same cultural things. Makes for a dull world and it also would be a weakness. Just like a hearty gene pool, the dynamic and diversified culture that is the American public is a rich fertile field of ideas, concepts and abilities. I don't want to lose that and that shouldn't be our goal.

I propose that what we need to do is become like minded on a large but simple "common" base. Establish the fact that we are Americans first and foremost. Sure, we can be different religions and races – but no matter what those topical difference are, at our core, we've all got to be on the same "American" team.

I want you to burn one thing into your mind. If you finish this book and remember nothing else, please remember this simple phrase...

"We The People"

The first three words of Our Constitution, the most powerful document concerning a nation on earth, starts with this phrase, right there in the preamble:

We the People of the United States, in Order to form a more perfect Union, establish Justice, insure domestic Tranquility, provide for the common defense, promote the general Welfare, and secure the Blessings of Liberty to ourselves and our Posterity, do ordain and establish this Constitution for the United States of America.

Can you understand that? Not just the preamble but the tone and definition of what's going on here. Thomas Jefferson wrote this (He and the Constitutional committees, but he gets most of the credit.)

Here's where so many people get lost. Jefferson, at that time, was not in Public Office – not by the standards of today. He wasn't in Federal Government because when this was written there was no Constitutional Federal Government – that's why they were writing a Constitution in the first place – to establish this new government.

Jefferson (although a statesman and well known) was just a regular "Joe". He wasn't a historical figure or a future President (like we know of him now) – he was just a guy. He was one of "The People".

He was a farmer and an architect. He had a regular job and duties to his family and farm. He hung out with his friends. He goofed off in his spare time. (Okay, he wasn't goofing off – he was inventing. But I bet there was some horseshoe playing and goofing off in there somewhere...) All the things that we do today, Jefferson was doing then.

What made him and the others like him (who founded this country) so special is that they knew that things had to change and they took it upon themselves to make those changes. A huge point here worth remembering is that "The People" were alive and well, thinking and acting, before there was ever a U.S. Government!

They knew that the former rule of the states by Great Britain was not working. The laws and system of it were corrupt, it denied people liberty and freedom and mostly it was just archaic and tyrannical. The founding Fathers of this country knew that, not only did this type of government have to go, but they also knew that they could start with a clean sheet of paper and build something fantastic!

Setting up a government is no easy task – especially one like they envisioned. Undaunted, they folded it together and cobbled this thing out of the most basic ideas.

America then, not unlike today, was populated by a very diverse set of cultures and subcultures. Trying to weave all of these different pieces together would be an impossibility. There were too many differing types of people, backgrounds, cultures and religions – so they came up with a stroke of genius – establish a government who's sole purpose is to bind the country together at the National level. Let the states make their own laws, let the communities and townships do the same and let each level answer to the level above as long as that level had the authority to request an answer.

For instance, a Federal law covered the entire Nation. State laws controlled the the State level down but not up. Local laws covered the local area on down but not the State or Federal level.

This way, the Federal government didn't have to get bogged down in controlling the states individually or at a granular, community level. This way the Federal Government didn't have to worry about governing the individual or trying to address the particular needs of an individual. This allowed the individual freedoms and room in their lives for that diversity while allowing the Federal Government to remain a relatively small and compact size – simply binding the states together. A Republic was born!

The real brilliant part of this were the interlocks built into the Constitution. The Constitution, by it's writing, is clear that a large, overpowering Federal Government would never work, so it also made clear that it could not interfere with the operation of states except where those few Federal laws were concerned.

Each state was required to set up it's own constitution and that each state would be responsible for conducting it's own government business and would have representation and a voice in the Federal Government on Federal Government and multi-state issues.

In short – those who wrote the Constitution wanted you to enjoy every freedom and liberty you could have, with a minimal amount of Federal laws and intervention – thus enabling you to grow, prosper, worship, speak your mind, travel and trade any way you thought best.

They knew that our diversity as a people, with all of our varied backgrounds and abilities with an absolute minimum of interference from the Government was the best chance of success and survival for our country.

It was a far stretch and many around the world waited for our failure. Because, on top of all this, the Constitution makes it very clear that the people (WE THE PEOPLE) would run our own government. That the government would answer to us and that we would control it. The great experiment, of a people run government, had begun.

Jefferson and the others prayed then for what we so blindly take for granted (and have nearly let slip because of our apathy). They wanted all this diversity to be able to come together, to grow and to survive. To be larger than life and for all people in our country to be able to meld these differences and, at the core, become one nation and a shining example to the world for liberty and freedom.

Think of that, knowing that we are diversified, but using our diversity as a strength! That no matter where we came from, our backgrounds and beliefs, that we would – at our core – be one. We would always be AMERICANS!

Many, many years ago, this was probably a very common thought and one that helped build this country into the great society that it is. Think of the powerful bond and strength they must have felt. Their pride and passion as a single people combined into one Nation. We the People!

Today that idea(l) seems so distant, so rare. In my lifetime, I've only seen one example of this "We are America - come hell or high water" spirit. That day?

September 12th, 2001.

September 11th, 2001 will live in many of our minds forever. Rather than launch into a history lesson it is sufficient to say that that day was absolutely horrible. There was only one benefit from this travesty. The following day...

On September 12th we woke up as a unified people. There were no races, no politics, no special interests – we were all simply

Americans – together stunned at what had happened. For a brief moment in time there was no issue over gun control, abortion, religion or race. Just a ticked off group of patriots ready to plant a flag everywhere you could find an open spot. America had been wronged and struck at on our own soil.

We were hurt, damaged – but our patriotism came back to us like the Prodigal Son. For a long time after September 12th, the spirit of America was overwhelming. We worried together, we pulled together, we prayed together... we shined together.

Then, sadly, over time the feeling wore off. It didn't take many months for the media to start it's usual spinning and for congress to start worrying about their voter base depending on which political/social group was waning tired of the Iraq effort and terrorist talk. Then, ultimately, the politicians got back to business as usual with fervor. Arguing over troop funding, to surge or not to surge, The Patriot Act, the treatment of captured terrorists, etc.

It has dawned on me that the terrorists had struck the wrong target at the wrong time. If they wanted desperately to upset Americans, there weren't many around on the September 11th. It's a shame that it took an act of powerful cowardice and destruction to bring our patriotism back out of hiding. I only wish the feeling had lasted a bit longer.

What I propose is that we recapture and maintain that common thread that we found for a brief time after the terrorists attacks.

Where we become color blind, religion blind, save the whales blind.... where we establish and maintain the common threads of all Americans. A set of threads that bind us together come "hell or high water" and we act on that in our decision making and in our actions as a unified people every day!

It's going to take that understanding and effort if the people are to ever regain what is rightfully, constitutionally theirs – their country, freedoms and their government.

We bicker, far too much and act terribly out of character to be a "people" as great as we pride ourselves upon being. We spout off and act upon things that we just socially "assume" are our rights as Americans and other times we fuss over points that aren't even supported by the Constitution at all.

I want to point a few of those out to you . These are all things that should reflect our collective "core" so to speak as Americans. There are many issues that, as a people, we need to address amongst ourselves. We need to grow up and act right and not continue to divide our own selves (the politicians do enough of that for us.).

Some of the following may hit a nerve with you and tick you off royally. If it hits a sore spot, check your mirror first before you come out swinging. We have to have unity and commonality as a liberty loving people and it has to be at the base level of our existence as a nation.

Remember, the things I'm pointing out are helping to keep us divided in this nation. The points were hardened and twisted by those pandering for votes and wanting to achieve and maintain their voice and power while reducing ours. If we all find agreement on these common points, imagine the high level of impact and political deflation it would have on politicians and their grip on us as a people. We can't stop them from dividing us if we don't stop dividing ourselves.

NO MORE PARTY LINES

No one should ever have to "reach across the aisle...", anymore. Ever. We are ALL Americans and to have any success at this - that old rhetoric HAS to go out the window!

The two party system (or for that matter – the multiple party system) was originally used as a "check and balance system" so that the internal bodies of Congress and the House of Representatives didn't just go loose and overrule the inner workings of government by overriding everything, voting one way and shoving their agenda down our collective throats.

In theory, the multiparty system is a really good idea. Fact is, it's been twisted to pieces and abused so much that (as it functions today) single party allegiance by a voter is pretty useless. Here's a perfect example of this:

Joe Lieberman. A Jewish Democrat (now an Independent) could quite possibly have gotten my vote for President had he made it that far in the primaries. At the political definition of the man – and conventional thinking - that should never happen where I'm concerned as a voter.

I'm a Conservative Christian. At first blush – I've got nothing in common with this man. But.... Mr. Lieberman has a conscious and he doesn't always vote based on his political party definitions.

He supported the efforts against terrorism, he's clearly a great family man, he speaks well of our country, he has some serious conservative thoughts rolling through his head and he obviously is a God fearing man. He does what he thinks is right and not always what the polls may say is popular for the moment. In the end, Joe Lieberman thinks about the impact of his actions upon his country and his fellow citizens before he makes a move. Good man.

Do I agree with every decision he's ever made? No way. But at the end of the day I feel confident that he will do what he deems best and will do it with a great regard for God and Country and not just his political gain. Yes, I could have voted for him and done so with a blind eye toward his political party affiliation. Much the same way that you would want to be treated based on your race, sex or religion when applying for a job. Just do good work, be the best applicant/candidate and let it go from there.

Any time we find ourselves voting for someone based on *any* factor besides their character, record and performance – we're begging for trouble.

NO MORE HYPHENATED AMERICANS

If you consider yourself African-American, Irish-American, Hispanic-American, etc. Then buy yourself a one way ticket back to the country of your roots and enjoy the trip.

You are welcome (and encouraged) to celebrate your culture and to share the best of it with all of us. But first, you are, and are expected to be, an American - plain and simple. This is the land of the *free*. And if you are that torn, then feel *free* to take your confused and divided self to the nearest exit.

This hyphenated business is stupid and it's just another one of those "divide the culture down into sub-groups" that the "progressives" in Washington just love! Sure, they want you to be an American so they can have your vote, but they want you to be a "hyphenated American" so they can pander and build a program directly suited for you and your "hyphenated" group alone.

Look, it's this simple – as a group, "Americans" aren't a minority. But, if they have us all watered down into our own little labeled "pocket groups" then we all, every one of us, fit into some form of minority classification and are weakened because of it.

If you're black there's no doubt that you have genetic roots in Africa. No question. But the great majority of black people in this country have never even been to Africa, and have no interest in going there to live. Point is, while my ancestry is from Italy, I've never wanted to call myself Italian-American.

I live here. My family and friends are here. It in no way diminishes me to not label myself as Italian. I'm sure Italy is a pretty place, probably has some fantastic people and scenery and I bet that the food is outstanding! But I have no desire to live there or call it home. There's no way that anywhere else, on it's best day, is better than my America on its' worst.

On top of that (I swear I'm not singling out my fellow Americans who are black) when it comes to minorities, there are many fewer Italian descendents in this country than there are African descendents. But you don't see the government pandering to me and offering me some carrot on a stick. Me and my kind can't generate enough votes as a group. So while I'm in a greater (smaller?) minority than so called "African-Americans" - I don't really count as a worthy target for their political efforts.

Bottom line? If you hyphenate your status as an American – you're being used as a chump by the politicians. They want and need you to do that and they are working you and your kind with everything they've got. Don't let them do that to you! Learn this valuable lesson: You are worth more and have more power as an American that you do as a hyphenated American.

(As a "fun" little footnote: If you believe the writings of the Bible and look at the supposed location of the Garden of Eden – we are ALL "Africans"! Let that soak in for a minute.)

LEARN THE NATIONAL ANTHEM AND THE PLEDGE OF ALLEGIANCE

Sing and say them and get the words right. It's what AMERICANS do. It's the saddest thing in the world to watch a sporting event and see someone flubbing this song.

It's a beautiful tune with fantastic lyrics and it's really simple to learn. Now granted, it's a toughie to sing – but even if your voice is as bad as mine – belt it out! It's like me being in a church – I feel so sorry for the poor souls next to me when I sing. I'm just pitiful. However, a choir director once told me – it's not your ability that matters – it's whether you feel it in your heart. And I do! ..with the comical grins and chagrin of my church going neighbors. I just butcher those poor hymns.

Same goes with "The Star Spangled Banner". Let it rip! Learn the words (which are included for you in the reference section at the end of this book) and sing them proud.

While you're doing that, also practice the proper etiquette of partaking in the singing of the National Anthem and the Pledge of Allegiance. Nothing looks worse on television than to see our so called sport "hero's" talking or blowing bubbles during this song! Man that lights my fire!

Take your hat off, stand or sit as erect as you can and let the world know that you are a proud part of those fortunate enough to be in the land of the free and the home of the brave!

PRAYER AND RESPECT

When the Pledge is said, the Anthem sang and a prayer is offered – partake. No hesitation, no cell phone calls, no running around. Get still, have some reverence and show some respect.

If the prayer or praying is offensive to you, then sit quietly and let the *majority* enjoy their freedom to do so.

If you want to be ugly about it, gripe and write a letter to someone saying that a prayer or a religious display or an icon is offensive to you then kindly leave the country. (See the "NO MORE HYPHENATED AMERICANS entry for instructions on how to do this. If you can't find the exit from America, I have millions of friends who will volunteer to show you to the door.)

You see, you certainly are entitled to and have every right in this country not to participate in prayer... *but*, those who choose too freely can participate and, at the end of the day, it's the *American Way* to pray. It's what we do.

We're fine if you choose not to - just have some respect. Even folks who don't pray can act as a good neighbor/citizen and behave as though their mother raised them properly. Just remember, that you have a choice and so do I . But as Americans it requires mutual respect from everyone so that both of us can exercise and enjoy our freedoms.

Also, and this is a BIG also – Remember that someone whom neither of us has ever met took a bullet so that I can pray and that you don't have to. They gave their life for us both to be able to choose. If you won't respect me and my mutual freedoms – at least respect that!

As far as participating in the Pledge of Allegiance and the National Anthem - you had better do that part at a minimum. Because that Anthem and that Flag represent the country that allows you the freedom to choose for yourself whether you pray or not.

FREEDOM OF SPEECH

Clear as a bell in the United States Constitution but don't forget the important aspects of it. Saying something doesn't make you an authority and, while no one has the authority to blockade or squelch your speech – you are not guaranteed an audience.

This is why we all have to be on vanguard for the politicians when they start singling out individuals who are speaking their minds or start going on about demanding "equal time" in the media. Those mediums are free enterprise systems (with the exception of Public Radio and Television) and cannot survive without selling advertisements. Long story short – if you can't stand talk radio or the hosts that have those shows, then you need to consider how they are able to stay on the air.

First of all the Constitution allows it and provides for it. It's a guarantee to their freedoms as a citizen. Try as they might with rule twisting or flexing their authority as an agency (the FCC), freedom of speech is a right. Period.

Secondly, since it's a free market activity – radio stations would pull these personalities off the air in an instant if no one cared to listen. With no listeners, there's no one sitting by and hearing the commercials. No one listening to commercials – the stations can't make money. If a show isn't making them money then off the air they go. End of story.

So, if you don't like Rush Limbaugh, Neil Boortz, Sean Hannity, Glenn Beck, Levin, etc. Stop whining. The larger portion of America does, is listening and the stations have the ratings and advertisers to prove it. Remember, your radio, television and computers all have off switches. Those guys aren't guaranteed an audience anymore than you are. But, if you're inclined, take a listen – you might learn something. If not, it's a free country, grab an off switch. It's your choice.

Also remember that while you have freedom of speech – it is to be done peacefully and assembled without strife. You can't take 100 friends with weapons and protest signs and run down the streets terrorizing everything. You may be right as rain, but the American public or military will make Swiss cheese out of you before your message is ever heard.

This book is an open statement to the public – but it's done as an offering and with every peaceful action and thought I can muster. I've said it many times that we must do something – but remember that this book is clearly a call to "action" and not "arms".

In short – speak your peace – calmly and firmly but do so with some intellect about your message.

POLITICAL CORRECTNESS

Another social/politician trick (mostly of the so called "Progressives"). This time they were so bold as to put their name on it - "*Political*" Correctness.

Let's face it, there are Mexicans in this world. There are bald people. People are fat. People are handicapped... the list goes on. Political Correctness (PC) is just a side stepping measure where you and I are expected to not really say what something is. Like saying that a midget is one of the "little people" - and not ever consider uttering the terrible word "midget". The supposed goal of this social tactic is to help knock off the rough edges of our "insensitivity" towards others. However, it doesn't really work.

Ultimately, all political correctness does is to further sub divide everyone down into more and more "special interest groups" that are sensitive to the "labels" they have been branded with from the rest of the "regular" society. This whole idea never really passes muster.

There is no such thing as a "regular" member of society or an "average" American. We come from all over, we have different backgrounds, we have different likes and dislikes, we are different heights, weights and sizes and we have differing mental and emotional capabilities. It's just a fact of life. A child with special needs could surely be considered a "Special Needs Child" - but that child is also mentally retarded. It's not a "label", it's not slanderous, it's just a fact.

The crux behind this and the "PC" way of thinking is the fear that factual words used to describe someone or something could be interpreted wrongly or taken as offensive by them. It's also a way of hiding fact. Just the other day I heard someone say that the term "socialist" was the new "N" word. Pushing the PC wagon around is a neat little trick to try and strike even accurate labels from our vernacular.

We've got to get past that because my human experience has taught me that people can, and will, take anything, any way, they please no matter what my actual words or intent were.

This is nothing more than a "progressive" social trick designed to make someone a "victim" any time that someone else "labels" them by doing nothing more than being descriptively accurate.

How dare I refer to a retarded child as retarded?

Then there are issues like the aforementioned ""N" word". Merriam-Webster does a great job on this one. It tells me that *"that word"* is considered to be one of the most offensive words in the English language, but, not necessarily when black people use it in referring to themselves or other black people.

That's one of the most ridiculous things I've ever heard. I've had black friends laugh at me and tell me that I don't "get it". They're right. I DON'T GET IT!

We can't have duality with each other as Americans. We can't have one set of rules for one type of person and another set for another. If black folks fought so hard for "equality" then why use a word to refer to themselves that's considered so degrading and offensive and reminiscent of their oppression? Bottom line, there's no justice to any of us in having two sets of rules for anything. Here's a great suggestion: Drop that "N" word and welcome to America!

That's part of the myth that Capitol Hill, politicians *and attorneys* want (and need) for us all to buy into. Seriously, are we supposed to revel in our diversity and then swat those that dare point out to us that we're not all the same?

We're all different. You know that and I know that – but if we all visibly recognize that fact, the law writers and vote mongers lose some of their leverage and ability to pander to the poor downtrodden little souls that need them for protection. The fact is, some people are just jerks and will always shoot off their mouth just being... well, a jerk! Remember what we teach our children about "Sticks and Stones..." We need to quit worrying about our toes getting stepped on and quit helping those who would like us to be divided.

Political correctness... you need to go bye bye!

SPEAKING ENGLISH

This one sets off a political bomb or two every so often and there's no reason for it in the world. Let me make this emphatically clear – WE SPEAK ENGLISH IN AMERICA!

This is so painfully obvious that we should instantly remove anyone from office if they vacillate on this subject at all.

The only reason politicians even consider allowances for any other language than English in this country is to pander to those non English Speaking (sometimes illegal) voters. Period.

With that, let me give you several points to ponder to reinforce your understanding and to give you some talking points the next time this comes up over coffee or beer.

- The U.S. Constitution – English.

- This country was founded by English speaking people. Other countries had their chance at owning territories and lost. They took their broken armies and their languages back home with them.

- Considering the use of another language is a slap in the face to those immigrants that came to this country and busted their humps to learn the English language. While it may come natural to most of us, English is a very tough language to learn and master.

- It's a gigantic waste of time to sit through a menu system on the phone and have to select whether I want English or Spanish. Clearly businesses are making good money too by pandering their wares to those that speak Spanish. (If it's possible, gripe to someone about this and don't do business with them anymore.)

- Our government buildings, other than the occasional flourish of Latin, are labeled, marked and named in English.

I've got a great system for deciding what language you need to speak no matter where you are in the world. Get a job. Wait until payday and cash your check. Now, look at the money you were handed. Whatever language the money is printed in – that's the language you should be using while you're there. Simple as that.

One America, one language, Liberty and Justice for ALL!

QUOTA FILLING

While I heartily agree that no one should be judged on their race, sex, religion, etc. to apply for a job – it's a stupid practice to force a business to fill some sort of quota based on those same factors.

Truth is, businesses are like a living organism. It relies on being as powerful and efficient as possible in order to survive and, hopefully, grow. Hiring the best of the best is critical in a business and having to make sure that 3 out of 10 openings (or whatever the current ratio is) are filled by any dolt who just happens to be of the right special interest group (despite their lack of qualifications or abilities) is just stupid. There's no other way to put it, it's stupid!

This is the work of the "brain surgeons**" in Washington again. Working both sides of it and keeping the pot stirred. (**I apologize to all of the Brain Surgeons in our audience.)

Let's be honest... If you are one of those people who was hired into a position just to fill a government demanded quota – your co-workers and bosses detest you! You may be a hard worker, you might be the greatest, most lovable person in the world – you may save a child on the way home from work – but they can't stand you!

Why? It's human nature (and it goes against good American values). Nobody likes anyone who gets special privileges. Nobody. Don't believe that? Then set a kindergarten class down and tell everyone in there that little Johnny is going to get something special just because he is wearing green shoes today. It won't be pretty for Johnny on the playground.

It's not only un-American but it's just downright rude and poor taste to allow this to happen. Sure we all want a break occasionally, but you are never doing yourself, your co-workers, friends, family or bosses a favor by accepting special treatment. It's demeaning to you especially when you let this happen and worse, it's a slap in your face by the politicians that enabled and enforce this.

In short, politicians are saying that minorities can't hack it if they have to get a job based on their abilities, test scores, etc. They need everyone's "charity" to make it in this world. So –

Mr. or Ms. Business owner, you must hire them and fill your "quota" because it's the right, charitable and ethical thing to do.

Says who? Not someone that has ever run a business or had to make a business survive in a competitive world.

Politicians say it's fair because it's spread out fairly and evenly amongst all businesses so what's the damage? Plenty.

Considering that small businesses are the backbone of our economy, are we to suggest that it's okay to weaken any one of them by being forced to hire unqualified people? Again, this is one stupid policy. It's damaging to free enterprise and businesses, it's degrading to those it supposedly is designed to help and it creates animosity amongst those employees who have to work side by side with these people every day.

There's no "justice" in this system. Business are compromised and, equally as important, unqualified job applicants are hurt because they have been given a "free pass". You never help someone by letting them advance when their skills aren't up to par.

Go take some some flying lessons and let's just see what happens when someone forces the instructor to "give you a pass" and lets you solo before you have the proper skills.

In the end? This lacks "excellence" and is also *crappy and consistent"* .

SEPERATION OF CHURCH AND STATE

We hear this one a lot and it always brings the house down. Politicians love this turmoil and every time I hear this phrase and the Constitution mentioned together I just cringe.

Let me make this very clear for you. Nowhere in the Constitution does it mention anything that resembles the phrase "Separation of Church and State". As a matter of fact, there's nothing in the Constitution that resembles that phrase, or even that idea, at all.

What people are wrongly referring to is the 1ˢᵗ Amendment, which is actually included in the "Bill of Rights". While not technically part of the original Constitution, that phrase still isn't even alluded to here either. Here's what it actually says in the 1ˢᵗ Amendment concerning religion...

"Congress shall make no law respecting an establishment of religion, or prohibiting the free exercise thereof..."

Pretty simple – just like the whole Constitution and it's supporting documents. Despite the wranglings and twisting of lawmakers and vote mongers, public myth or opinion – it's as plain as day.

Congress will not (cannot) make any law establishing a religion, including a state (government) run religion. Also, they will never be allowed to make a law limiting or prohibiting your freedom to participate (or not) in any religion you choose.

Period. There you have it, right before your eyes. If you can find some magical way to read that any differently – then I'd like to know how.

Congress could try all they want to control religion, but the Constitution denies them that authority no matter how much they, or any voter, would like.

Having said that, it does not in any way go against the Constitution or suggest establishing a religion by printing "In God We Trust" on our money. The 1ˢᵗ Amendment doesn't prevent prayer in schools (yes, even public schools). It doesn't stop the 10 commandments from appearing in a courtroom (there are copies of it embedded in the woodwork in the Supreme Court building and on it's friezes outside.).

Fact is, the whole issue, Constitutionally is a dead fish.

We are a God fearing and believing country. We pray. We talk about God and religion. It's always been that way and honestly, that never needs to change. You don't have to acknowledge that fact or participate if you don't want to. The Constitution provides for that as well. But every now and again you hear about someone losing their mind for being offended by a Nativity scene during Christmas.

Anytime you hear someone going on about this, you can rest assured that they either know nothing about the Constitution or they really do understand it and just want to try and trim back your liberties a bit more over nothing more than fluff.

Those that have been infringed upon in any way (had their religious liberties stepped on) by this issue need to vote into office some people who can read and comprehend.

That's why I tell you to know your Constitution.

INNOCENT UNTIL PROVEN GUILTY

I've heard many people refer to this as being in the Constitution as well. It isn't. Nowhere is this phrase or idea within the Constitution of the United States.

The idea of this comes from "Jurisprudence" which is the foundation of our legal code and court system in America. Only a court of law in the U.S. must assume that you are innocent until proven guilty. It does not protect you from the vicious court of "public opinion" at all.

This is a sad example, but it's fresh, so I'll use it. If it strikes you as in poor taste, I heartily apologize.

During Michael Jackson's funeral (memorial service) a lady, quite upset and speaking out in defense of Mr. Jackson and some of his alleged unsavory accusations said something to the effect of, "People had been unfair to him. He's innocent until proven guilty.... we know the Constitution."

No they don't.

The sad truth is, people can be a mean spirited bunch. It's a bad social practice, assuming that someone is guilty without fact. Because that's selective and harmful to someones' character - especially if they're innocent.

I know that you can think of examples where the public had convinced themselves that a person was guilty of a crime who later was released from incarceration or suspicion because the real killer or culprit came forward. Peoples lives have been destroyed because of public opinion and public opinion alone.

A good practice for us all is to let the courts decide criminal matters and let's just pray that true justice is served.

Don't miss the bigger lesson here. Don't assume that you know what you think is right or what someone, a politician especially, is telling you. This is a thematic warning throughout this book. Get your facts because the powers that be can't deny or take from you something that you are knowledgeable of. Know your constitution, your rights, etc. and do a good inventory. You can count on the U.S. Constitution, but just like that poor lady at the Jackson funeral, don't feel falsely "protected" by something that isn't there as well.

LOVE A VETERAN

For that matter, extend courtesy to all of our uniformed men and women – whether they've seen combat duty or not.

Let's face it. Military life is tough. You are U.S. Government property while you serve. You are removed from life as a civilian and you may very well find yourself in terrible conditions risking your life.

The fact is, it's pretty much hell on earth.

These fine people volunteered for service and our military has always been voluntary (except for draft supplementation). In many countries, military service is required by every citizen at some time in their lives.

Our military is the finest in the world and the people who serve the U.S. Armed forces are absolute champions. They are simply the best.

The next time you meet someone who is serving or has served, reach out your hand and tell them "Thank You".

People who disrespect our military are not worthy of their protection or their services. But they extend it all the same. I've seen people verbally abuse our military and, with a ton of pride and grace, I've seen these soldiers just shrug it off. They should never have to do that. That's an embarrassment to everyone involved.

If you ever see this happen, stand up for that soldier. They have too much class to do so themselves. But it breaks my heart to see these people - who will go out and defend this country or defend the country of another - not be able to defend their own pride to a fellow U.S. Citizen.

You don't have to agree with policy or even the military efforts these men and women are sent to carry out – but you had better defend that soldier! Tell your Government Representatives to fund them and fund them well! They may be an Army of one – but I want each and every "one" of them armed, armored and comfortable. I want them backed up with support so that they are always fresh, rested and able to carry out their duties with every advantage possible.

While I've talked about several issues in this book and have offered some debate, this isn't one of them!

Under no circumstance ever let your politicians undercut our soldiers or our military. Theses people and these services aren't some water fountain at a park or any other "special interest" project.

The Constitution requires Congress to provide us with a well funded military. See to it, as a fellow American, that we don't let this slip. As I just mentioned, I want my servicemen and servicewomen (and their families) as comfortable, well fed, well paid and more able to perform their duties than anyone else in the world.

They spend life away from home. Away from their children, spouses, family and friends to fight for liberty and protect your right to gripe. Respect them and take care of them!

I always want the world to know that you can have no better friend or a worse enemy than a U.S. Soldier. God bless them.

In short, it's up to us to vanguard our individual liberties in this country and never become divided over our little social issues. We have plenty on our plate to fix within our government and we may as well address our social problems right along with it.

Stop being so spineless and foolish.

Every time you hear a politician having to "sell" us on an idea or watch them defend some political issue – throw up a warning flag. Remember, they need our little heads down cobbling over all the "noise" we let them generate. All the little laws and regulations that fly in the face of common sense. It's part of their "tricks". Don't go there. Just like in sports, keep your eyes on the prize!

Push back against the temptation to think about your personal issues. Let's pool our efforts and fight for the big ones, our liberties!

Watch out for your fellow American too. When you see one of them becoming a self inflicted victim, talk to them and have them reconsider. Help them to understand and rise above the trickery that's being offered to them. Remember, their pain is a politicians gain!

We need to help those who have stumbled – get them out of the way from the wheels of the bus. The politicians will roll right over them in the name of "good will" only to suck them into their system of pandering and vote fishing.

Heads high everyone! Special laws for special interest be damned! Liberty, justice – it's what we're made of. There's no justice in an underfunded military. There's no liberty in being handed a job because you help fill a quota! Demand excellence and demand REAL equality for us all. Know your Constitution for yourself and quit letting someone who needs your vote dictate to you what your true freedoms are! Get strong, be proud and be AMERICANS!

When we, the American people, as one "We the People", finally take our country back, then – and only then - can we have true Liberty and Justice for all!

CHAPTER

5

The Plan

Let's get straight to this. So far in this book I've gone over two important themes. One, that we are a great people with God given rights to liberty and freedom and Two, the goal of those that wish to take these rights from us is to keep us busy and stirred while they do their dirty work.

The idea here was to get you to look at these political tactics and understand them. Because it's important to look upon those in Government who are doing this as the enemy and the best way to defeat an enemy is to understand them thoroughly.

Also, I'd like to offer some advice about the idea of a "plan" in general. A plan, once laid out becomes a given, a subscribed course of action. Plans generally lack flexibility because large parts of them require exact precision at certain key times and points.

For our goals I don't think that's wise.

For instance, Communism required a set of writings (A Communist Manifesto), Hitler and Mao both had their little "books" that detailed their plans.

Evil and tyranny always have a "plan" - that is its' failing. Because it's so rigid the core values and the ingenuity of the people and their want for freedom once trapped by their "plan" - will always undo it. The arrogance of evil will always be it's undoing.

As Americans we have ingenuity and a love of freedom. So in our little book, we won't set a "hard" rigid plan.

Instead, let's lay down some guidelines and suggestions, just like a certain Constitution I'm so fond of, and work from there.

Here we go!

- **Get your heart right.**
- **Wise up and get smart.**
- **Walk with Liberty.**
- **Be charitable.**
- **Become Solvent.**
- **Be Brave.**
- **Speak your mind.**
- **Help others.**
- **Vote.**
- **Watch.**

Get your heart right.

Remember when I talked about being a great American? All those points about things you should do in your community. Now is the time to put some of that into action. I can recommend a thousand things you could do, but it goes so much deeper than that.

Get "YOU" right as well. Drinking or drug problem? Get rid of it. It's a waste of time. If you have emotional problems or other personal issues, address them. We need every able bodied person helping out for the efforts. If that won't inspire you enough then do it for yourself and the people who love you.

Feel alone? Don't.

Someone reading this book is looking for someone to talk with about it and it may be you!

Rediscover family. Get the kids to actually sit at the dinner table. Put away the cell phones and turn off the internet and the television. Learn to talk with and care about one another again. As your children get older they are going to need a good base to build their core values and lives on. Provide it for them. You can't beat family!

If you don't have a family, borrow one! Be a good enough neighbor so that you can be invited along with others. Fellowship is critical not only for our mental health but for our society as well. In the same measure, if you see someone who is alone or a family without a Mom or a Dad – help them out and get them involved. Let folks know that you want to be cared about and that you'll also care about them.

Learn to pray. If you never have, then start. If you do pray, then pray more. Don't pray for God to provide a fix – but to help give you the guidance and wisdom to do good works for yourself and others and to find the strength and tools to fight for liberty.

Lastly, open up your heart and get past your prejudices, bias or angers. Have you been discriminated against? Don't cry – it happens to all of us on some levels. Just seek those who seek you – as an equal, as an American.

There are plenty of politicians who will offer you "social salvation". Leave it alone! It's a trap. Let your fellow Americans come to your aid. And believe me, they will! As Americans we need everyone, big or small from every race, creed and religion to come together and stand together. DO IT!

Every society has jerks. Don't be one and don't give those who are a free pass. The good group of folks will be larger than the jerks. I guarantee it! Stand together.

Get your heart right on these things or the political powers that be will try to suck you back in to their "protection". Don't be helpless and dependent upon them and their hoax. Only we can love and nurture each other!

Wise up and Get Smart

Politicians are reliant upon our apathy and confusion on issues. No more of this! I've shown you a few of their "tricks" in this book, but believe me, they have a million of them.

Pull your nose out of the Supermarket tabloids and start watching, and studying, the news. All the networks that you can. A different one every day. Pretty soon you will begin to see who's being honest in the media and who isn't. Who's telling all the sides of the story and if there's a slant as to what they say. I have my personal favorites, but I still watch them all. I enjoy seeing who's butt-kissing and how they're doing it.

Then comes the next step in the logic. Why?

Why is there a slant in some media outlets? Shouldn't the news be just that? The news? Straight reporting of the facts. This question alone will force you to start looking into the news yourself. The simple idea that there are two or more variations on the same story and the facts is clear evidence that something is amiss here. Curiosity will get the best of you and you'll start digging and fact finding on your own.

Eventually you will develop an eye and an ear for both the media and what's happening in the world. Follow your gut instinct. Always ask "why?". Be like a little kid. A kid will ask you why the sky is blue and "why, why, why" you all the way back through physics, chemistry, the "big bang" and God's original plan for the universe. (Man they're cute but they can be exhaustive on stuff like this!)

Don't let the politicians prey on your stupidity. Do yourself a favor. Be a kid.... and be smart.

Walk with Liberty

Get to know your Constitution (I've included a copy in this book) because it's your friend. Doesn't take long to read and it'll really open up your eyes!

Once you see how simple and bold it is you'll be able to see the multitude of ways that it has been twisted and put upon. People say that it's a "living" document. No it's not. It was set in stone at the cost of a ton of blood.

Our laws in this country, for the most part, are not unconstitutional. But what the law does is snip away at our rights until all we have left is basically the core only. That's confining, doesn't allow true freedom of choices and is, by the written Constitution... unconstitutional.

Get down to the library or bookstore and get loaded up with American history and writings. Not political memoirs by Bill Clinton or one of the Bush's – go for Jefferson, Washington, Franklin... start with that. Learn about the Federalist papers and see what was brewing when they wrote the Constitution. Get that locked into your brain. Then, if you like, read up on the more modern Presidents.

Memoirs are great – but I'd recommend the history first. If you liked Carter or Reagan and are a fan – knock yourself out – but biographies tend to smooth over the real history and are nothing compared to a Congressional and Presidential record of who voted for what. History and their personal ethics will tell you why.

Once you have some background on the history of things begin to couple that with "Being Smart".

If you do this, you'll quickly see a trail of how we got from "there" to "here". Trust me, it's not pretty – but at least you'll be armed with the knowledge of how rotten some of this has been and you'll be a lot wiser. Now that you are "armed" with a good brain and heart, let's put it to work!

Be Charitable

Like they used to say in the old church. "Give 'till it hurts!". Well, that's the idea. But I'm not just talking about money.

Sure, giving to a charity is always a great idea – but you should be doing that with the first step under "Get(ting) Your Heart Right".

The biggest one I want you to do is to approach your social and political "opposition" with open arms and a heart. President Obama has told his supporters that when it comes to discussing his health plan with those that oppose it to "Get up in their face, argue with them" and "...if they bring a knife, you bring a gun!". I believe that's mostly metaphorical – but he's certainly not suggesting an environment that's readily open for intelligent debate. Thanks Mr. President, you're really incubating a great new movement there. (Not the kind of "Change" for America I'm looking for.)

Let's be honest here. These policies, this government and that kind of thinking and approach from his followers is wrong. They'll find out soon enough that these tactics will fail with a freedom loving people. Until then, have some love for your fellow man, while they may not realize it yet, they're in this mess too.

Use your newly found knowledge and let them squawk just like the "faulty" network news reporting. Then, ask them questions.

Interview them. Don't argue. Remember, you're simply trying to find the facts that all Americans should be entitled to. Press them on it. They did all the talking and the squawking and YOU are the bad guy (remember?).

So, let them talk – hear them – then ask them, very calmly, to tell you why you should change your mind.

When they have their facts wrong, don't just tell that they're wrong, ask them to consider your opinion. Give them a reference, something from a report, a news item, whatever.

Because the truth is that the White house and certain members of Congress and the Senate are lying to them. Plain and simple. They are not going to like admitting to this fact. Who can blame them? They have sold themselves to a lie machine and coming to grips with that is painful. (Remember our mirror in Chapter 1?)

Don't shove facts in their face just to be a wise guy. Offer, like a loving friend (and fellow American) guidance and the truth.

If they don't consider your points, it's their loss, and then, the burden is on them. They've been given honest fact from a caring fellow American. They will either come to study that on their own and appreciate you for your care and kindness or they'll just blow it off. Either way – you have done your duty and service and have offended and hurt no one by telling the truth.

Be charitable with your knowledge and heart!

Become Solvent.

This is a biggie! I'm not suggesting that you sell everything and live in a box. But, if you have to, then minimize. Stop that big house or car payment from hanging over your head. You'll be surprised on how little it actually takes to live. Trying to keep up with the Jones'? Don't. Let *them* go broke.

The U.S. Government (i.e. us too) is buried up to its' ears in bad debt. Trillions and trillions of dollars worth. We will never get our national debt paid off.

Imagine if this country were solvent (owed nothing to anyone) and we had a surplus of a trillion dollars in our coffers.

You want national healthcare? Okay, that money would be enough to buy each of us (that's EVERY man, woman and child in America) a health policy worth about $3000 a year. (That's $12,00 to $15,000 a year for an average size family policy). That should cover it nicely.

But we can't – so the Government just promises things and taxes us more and more to cover those promises. We pay for today both now and in the future.

Solvency teaches and proves fiscal responsibility and it's the only way to mathematically grow wealth.

Prove it to yourself. Look at your personal budget. Now remove every loan payment and credit card payment you have out of it. Now how much does it cost you to live? Very little! We need this country to be solvent as well.

Solvent, even on less money gives you great control over your destiny. Think how fast your personal wealth would grow with no bills staring you in your face? Imagine taking those monthly payments and using them for savings deposits instead!

Look at China. A communist country and they are (almost alone) paying for our TARP money (financial bailout) and national debt by them buying our bonds. What does that mean? Well in short, China owns us. In the future we will be bending our foreign policy and relations toward them and playing all "nice" because if they demanded immediate payment, we'd be in huge trouble. I guess we could just give them everything west of the Mississippi river.

The point being, get yourself in good financial shape. This will help you ride out the rough economic times and conditions you to be ready with money in hand in case we hit another bump in the road. Trust me, if your affairs are in order, you won't be so likely to allow Congress to throw them out of shape.

While you're at it, do some research on economics. If you do and you study the free market system a bit, you'll begin to see that "big business" isn't a "big problem" and exactly what government interference with it is costing us!

Be Brave

The following points in the plan require bravery – and not just the social kind. Here's where the tire hits the road.

You will have to develop your bravery. If town hall meetings of late have taught us anything it's that the status-quo counts on the American public being a bunch of needy little cowards who will take anything thrust upon them.

If you show up, you'll be threatened or muscled against. If you speak you'll be called anything but an American.

Pay no mind to this.

You are a "social soldier" for liberty and freedom. Not a weapon wielding anarchist – but a citizen of the United States who is guaranteed by the Constitution the freedom of speech. Anyone, and I mean anyone, who chastises you for exercising that freedom is nothing short being anti-American. Get it through your head – You are Constitutionally guaranteed the right to redress the government with a grievance.

It's one thing to debate a point with you – it's entirely another if they berate you for doing so. Any politician or public official who supports or arranges for you to be silenced should be removed from office immediately. Do you hear me? Immediately! Because if they do this, they are denying their support and belief in the U.S. Constitution. This goes against their oath of office and is an impeachable offense.

Don't let fear or threat stop you from being a patriot. They've got tactics – taxation, ridicule, threats, legal – you name it. But none of them hold water Constitutionally. Be brave – your fellow Americans and the Constitution have your back.

Speak Your Mind

Now you should have a working knowledge and lifestyle that's a model of what our government should be doing. You have a heart and a mind, with open arms allowing you to care for your neighbor, you're charitable and financially sound. You understand liberty and freedom.

Get it out on the street!!

Be a walking and talking "little America"! You know your rights and the rights of others. Speak up when someone has a little "issue" and decide if that issue is a "just" one or are they asking for special treatment or favoritism? We know that doesn't work.

Is there a way to network with your other Americans and get a problem solved – at the "people" level? Remember, we can do a great deal more than we realize if we just do a small part together. (Get the spoons!)

Know the full extent of your liberties as well as their boundaries. But act on them!

If someone needs a speaker for their group or someone needs somebody to talk about liberty and patriotism, speak up! You're as qualified as anyone else. (I mean, my gosh... look at me.) Sure, it's a blessing from God to be born an American, but operating on the principles of liberty is a learned task. Learn and show others! But speak up!

If you are at a rally or a town hall meeting and something doesn't sound right (gut feeling) raise your hand and politely ask questions. If the answer doesn't strike you right, continue to ask another question until your question is thoroughly answered. (Be a kid.) You'll be surprised how many folks around you were wondering as well and will appreciate you for your diligence.

Speaking comes with a price. You must also be willing to listen. But by all means do! Be open to the concept that good ideas can come from anywhere. CEO's and homeless people both can have some brilliant ideas! Get those ears open – but speak as well!

We need everyone with a good mind and heart that has done their homework to get those great ideas flowing. Out of these conversations and open exchanges we will find our new and improved leaders/public servants for those soon to be vacant seats in the government.

The last thing a politician wants is for someone with some brains to stand up and politely ask a pointed and unambiguous question. It takes them away from their "script" and forces them to truly do what any leader must do. Deal with real problems!

Ask them. Press for an intelligible answer. Don't let them sidestep or offer pacification. If you have to, call BS! But SPEAK!

Get your mind right and speak it – often!

Help Others

This isn't about doing charitable deeds or entertaining at the nursing home. This is about helping others become who and what you are as an American as well as part of the solution.

Not only do you need to incubate what you've now learned and are doing with your neighbors and fellow countrymen – I want you to teach it to our children and volunteer to help those who just got here.

The children part is probably easy. You may have children or grandchildren so they are nearby and dear to your heart already. But reach out further than that – and be creative too.

Can you pull off dressing up and acting like a historical figure – Ben Franklin or George Washington? How about a famous black or a female historic figure or some other character? Go for it! Make it a project too. Get someone to volunteer the material (authentic period clothes from our revolution are heavy and scratchy – so this will be a sacrifice) and do the sewing, you work on your lines and presentation. Take this to civic groups and schools. They'll love you and you'll be a hero to boot!

Help create great Americans! This is a fantastic way to do that and to help others learn the valuable information you now know.

The next few points may be a little tougher – but suck it up! We're Americans!

Help those who are freshly "hurt" that discovered that they've been lied to and help those who want to become American citizens.

Most of you are quite aware of the debacles I've referred to in this book concerning the state of confusion and, well... mutiny, that's going on in Washington today. This didn't happen by accident. A lot of good people gave up a perfectly good vote to help make this stupidity happen.

Since the approval ratings for many politicians are much lower than their vote percentages, it can only mean that there are a lot of good people really hacked off at their candidate.

Help these good people.

Don't beat them up for their decisions, just guide them through the same steps you've been through and let them know that we will ALL do a better job during the next election. Let them know that we are here for them and that, even when mistakes are made, we Americans stick together. (Prodigal Son from the Bible anyone?) When you help them, they will in turn help others. This is a win/win for everyone and for America.

Help those who want to become legal citizens of this country. As I said, I know this is tough because there's a boatload of prejudice and bias here. But hear me out.

It's a blessing from God to be born here. Despite our problems, I wouldn't want to live anywhere else. But imagine, if you will, how bad it would have to be for you to want to denounce your U.S. Citizenship and move you and your family to an entirely new country. Wouldn't that be heart wrenching? I shudder to think. But just imagine. That's what they've been through.

We have a huge problem with illegals in this country, both socially and financially and it tends to muddy the waters a bit on this. But there are many, many who are trying to gain legal citizenship for themselves. Help them! Because they are trying to become Americans during some of our darker hours.

Volunteer to teach English or Civics classes to these people. Be a mentor or just be a friend and help them in private with a little tutoring. Let them know first hand, from your experience, what's really going on in the country today. Don't let them be a target of pandering from a politician. Teach them to be a true independent and free American!

While a politician may try and "buy" their vote, teach them the value of having officials representing them that have "earned" that vote. Those rare politicians who will fight to keep a big government out of their way and never limit them or their potential. There's a difference and you owe them the facts. That's one less social "victim" on the streets and another "strong" American within our ranks.

Vote

Plain and simple... VOTE! Vote wisely and armed with knowledge.

I've heard so many people say that their vote doesn't matter or that it doesn't count. If that sounds like you then never, ever, say that again.

If you hear someone else say that, take them by the hand (seriously) look them in the eye and ask them this:

"If your vote doesn't count, then why are politicians willing to lie to you or buy you off in order to get it?"

Your vote is the same vote that every other American has. No matter their net worth, race or religion. It's the most powerful thing on this planet because it allows you a say in the course of the most powerful country in the world.

Never, and I mean NEVER, underestimate it's value.

What do you do with your vote? Whatever you choose. I draw the line there in this book and in my thinking. I would never dictate in a plan of freedom any instructions on how you should cast your vote!

But I give you this to consider when voting. If we have the people taking into consideration all the things I outlined in this book, we will soon have a Government full of Great Americans.

Ones who truly represent us, are listening to us and doing our bidding. Ones we can put on autopilot (to a degree) and let them watch the store while we continue on with our work and let the people get back to solving the problems of the people.

Vote, by all means vote, and I strongly recommend that we act like hawks watching out for and penalizing anyone or any group who tries to hamper or tamper with the process.

Knowing how powerful voting is and the impact tampering could have, it should be treated as treasonous if anyone violates the sanctity of that process. Full Federal imprisonment with nothing less than a life sentence for hampering or tampering with the voting process.

Serious? You bet!

Watch

Stay diligent and guard all that we have worked so hard to recover. Watch closely our newly elected people. Raise the roof if they so much as budge off course. Fight tooth and nail to be heard and correct them. If that fails – remove them from office. Immediately, if they breach the trust and oath of their position or remove them by vote during the next election cycle if they fail to perform.

Once politicians realize that we are ever diligent in watching them, they will think more than twice before they move their hand or before ever even running for an office.

No more funny business.

Continue on with the plan so that this never happens again. Teach this lesson to our children as well so they and their children never fall asleep and get suckered like we did!

Keep the plan alive! So watch your own self as well.

Follow it every day. Work off of our strengths and be strong.

We can not afford to be divided, because divided we fall (yes I said it again!). It's so true. We must forever be one nation of people, like minded on our most basic values and beliefs and exercising our freedoms and liberties.

This will work!

You see, the beauty of my "plan" and the goal of this book is simple... trust people with their true liberties and freedoms as instructed by the Founding Fathers and the U.S. Constitution.

I didn't come up with some great idea here. It was already there – we've just become so convoluted and distant from it that we lost our way. This isn't hard. It's actually very obvious. But recognizing it and correcting it have great benefits.

If we put the right people in office, those who bubble up from our true ranks as American people, we'll truly have a government that's of and by the people. We'll know that our new Government servants are working off our common thread, values, goals, hopes and ambitions.

The newly chosen will understand and will vanguard our liberties and freedoms. When we aren't tied down having to watchdog everything we can focus on our own social issues.

First of all, those issues will be fewer if we're all acting like Great Americans and secondly, as Americans, we can rest assured that our "people level" fixes will be much greater and more enduring than any government program ever could be.

I'll never ask anyone to "dumb down" their issues or compromise their freedoms and liberties to save this country. (You shouldn't have to.) But a big problem we have has been the habit of taking a major pain killer when a simple aspirin would do.

The concept of "Occams' Razor" holds true. The simplest solution is probably the right one. Let's keep it simple and honest. Something everyone can follow and see the simple beauty of.

Like I started this book, I don't care about political parties or personal beliefs – but there's no way that anyone who calls this land home, loves America and can read the Constitution can argue validly against such a simple proposal.

We, and the world need America strong! We need it's liberty. We need it's freedoms. We owe it to the world to fight and keep what's promised to us by our founding Fathers.

It's our collective inheritance but we can never just assume that it will be there for us. We must watch out for it every day and always hold those liberties with great regard and reverence. We can save it now, it's not too late, but once it's gone, it's gone.

Think about the plan and your part in it. Consider all that you can do and bring to the table. You aren't too old nor young, rich or poor, great or small. Like I said, I could care less who or what you are. Lady Liberty is no different. Just come to her with open hearts and minds and your honesty.

She'll do the rest.

CHAPTER

6

The "Test"

~or~

A Bonus Chapter Just for You!

People have asked my how is it that I have the "nose" I do for sniffing out a problem within the goings on in Capitol Hill?

I used to pride myself on thinking, foolishly that I just had a "gift" for it. You know, like I was somehow "magical". Easy enough to believe because my being able to spot a problem a mile away is eerily accurate.

This shocks most people because a lot of those so called prognosticators and pundits are the real paranoid "doom and gloom" types. Not me. I'm actually very laid back, positive about nearly everything and am, ultimately, a very fun loving guy. Still, my track record in this department is spot on.

I do the "gut" check very often on things and I've always just thought that I had clever guts – but I've also realized that many folks don't. And they have a genuine fear of finding out that a problem is a problem after it's too late. This further ramps up their fears and adds to their apathy. They feel that it's better to do nothing than to make a wrong move or risk taking a wrong stance on a topic.

Well, that's safe.... but unfortunately, that's playing right into the tactics of those who wish to keep you timid and small. Remember, politicians need you feel clumsy and somewhat afraid.

Well, I can't have that happen to you.

So I began to really study my gut instincts. (Not my gut itself, because every time I do that, I realize that I really need to do some sit ups and it just depresses me...) I had to acknowledge that behind every "magical" talent, there is, in fact, a process to it.

Dissecting a process allows you to prove that it's repeatable and recordable and ultimately makes it teachable. Like a great cake recipe. It's just a shareable, learnable, set of instructions. There are clear amounts of this or that combined a certain way that will always create a desired level of "cakey goodness"! And honestly, what's better than cake?

So, I set out to study this process so that you too can make a cake. (Metaphorically speaking at least.) Rather than go into a lengthy explanation of telling you how I worked all of this out (mostly sticky notes and observation), I will simply present the finished product to you.

With that, I give you a "bonus". Here are the instructions to the "Joey Bruno - Political BS" test!

The TEST!

When I hear a politician or some other Government "official" come out and say "Hey! Here's this new thing......." It gets the "test"! Here's how it's done:

First, listen to exactly what they are saying. Not what you want to hear or the incomplete parts you've heard. Find out EXACTLY WHAT THEY SAID. Be warned... Politicians are masters of word-speak and definition twisting and slant.

Get all the facts then run it all through this little filter in your head......

As defined within the U.S. Constitution:

Does this action in any way diminish the freedoms or independence of me, my Country or my fellow Americans?

Does this action in any way deny me the right to choose and have ultimate control over my own destiny?

Does this action in any way place a burden on others based on my actions or inaction?

Does this action in any way make someone besides myself the master of me, my belongings, my property or my livelihood?

Ultimately, Does this action deny me or my fellow Americans' their liberty?

That's it – nothing fancy and quite simple actually – but then again, it should be. All reliable things are simple.

Did you notice that I used the term *"in any way"* over and over in the test? That's a critical thing and it took me a while to realize the importance of it when I wrote this.

Why so important? Because politicians hate this! The term, "in any way", is a broad, broad blanket. Now, they (politicians) just l-o-v-e to use this when *they* are getting to do or decide something. "In any way" really closes up the gap when putting the screws to someone because it leaves no room for error or twisting. Politicians have a self given right to be vague while you must be exact. (They can have an "oops" on their taxes, you can't!)

So, knowing this about their character, I put it in my test. Because it's those little "exceptions" in everything they do that allow them to slip things into laws and chip away at our freedoms while gaining them another inch of authority and power over you.

Let's put it through it's paces really quick to show you how it works.

I'll use Welfare again as an example. It's been around a long time and most folks understand the system pretty well.

Here's the test in action! Remember, it's always "According to the Constitution".

Does this action in any way diminish the freedoms or independence of me, my Country or my fellow Americans?

At first glance no. It would appear outwardly to be for the benefit of someone who was having a hardship.

Does this action in any way deny me the right to choose and have ultimate control over my own destiny?

Not as a contributor. But as a recipient? Yes. A recipient has to ultimately answer to someone for the charity they are receiving from the state.

Does this action in any way place a burden on others based on my actions or inaction?

Yes. Again as a recipient, you are a burden on your fellow Americans who are paying taxes to be redistributed to you and the others on Welfare. The Constitution does not suggest or require that the people provide public welfare for others.

Does this action in any way make someone besides myself the master of me, my belongings, my property or my livelihood?

Again, Yes. Because ultimately, any property you may own that was purchased while you were on welfare was paid for in part or whole by the American people through their taxation.

Ultimately, Does this action deny me or my fellow Americans' their liberty.

Again, at first blush, no. But, after some thought you can easily see where this thing is a liberty killer. People become addicted to this system, sometimes relying on it as a lifestyle and totally removing themselves from their pursuit of happiness in this country. They are victims of their own growing apathy, but mostly by the politicians who wish to keep them trapped there, in poverty, as part of their dependent voting contingency.

As I've mentioned previously in the book, this isn't to say that welfare and charity are bad things in this country... not at all. But to have it as a Federal Policy and law coming out of our taxes?

No. Makes no sense. Doesn't pass the test.

Clearly something should always be done when one of our fellow Americans is in trouble. But honestly, does it require political and legal mandate for us to get this done? No.

Now take the same test and apply it to having to stop at a Stop sign. Passes with flying colors. Doesn't step on your toes or the toes of anyone else. It's certainly good for public safety. It doesn't violate constitutional policy, rights or freedoms. Done.

Now, take the test and apply it to any topic you choose. Feel free to modify the test for your own use and what works best with your "gut". But I do suggest that you keep the "*in any way*" term within your test too. In the end, if a topic passes through the test with no bumps – we're probably okay. If it hits a snag anywhere – watch out for your rights and freedoms. Something is afoot!

If I had a billion dollars I would print this test on business cards and mail them to everyone in the country. I'd end up on a political "black ball" list for sure. But, everyone would have a copy and could study up on these wise guys and their tactics.

So, since I can't just freely give one to everybody, I included it here for you.

For that matter, I hope you've enjoyed the book. It took a great deal of effort to put this little offering together, but it's been a great experience.

I only hope that you have found some value within its humble pages and that you may be inclined to tell others about it.

Now, go out there, be a Great American and walk proud as a Modern Day Patriot!!

CHAPTER

7

Final Thoughts

I've done my best to make a simple "ideal" into an "idea"... to try and make it as palatable as possible for the masses. A great writer, I am not. I've tried to stay on track, not do any political leaning nor let my own personal views get in the way of saying what I though *must* be said.

In all, what I do know is that we have to get back to just our core as being Americans, cast out our pettiness and put a stop to those who manipulate us over it. As clumsy a job as I may have done, that was my goal.

But in closing this book I am compelled to share with you my heart of hearts. Not everything mind you, but just my ramblings as I, with a great deal of fatigue, finally put our little book to rest.

During my notes and research for "Divided We Fall" let me share something with you that I had to read:

"When, in the course of development, class distinctions have disappeared, and all production has been concentrated in the hands of a vast association of the whole nation, the public power will lose its political character. Political power, properly so called, is merely the organized power of one class for oppressing another....."

That passage is concerning the "transition period" from a little document called the "Communist Manifesto" - literally a recipe for communism. Let me show you more from it:

10 Conditions For Transition To Communism

1. Abolition of property in land and application of all rents of land to public purposes.

2. A heavy progressive or graduated income tax.

3. Abolition of all right of inheritance.

4. Confiscation of the property of all emigrants and rebels.

5. Centralization of credit in the hands of the State, by means of a national bank with State capital and an exclusive monopoly.

6. Centralization of the means of communication and transport in the hands of the State.

7. Extension of factories and instruments of production owned by the State; the bringing into cultivation of waste-lands, and the improvement of the soil generally in accordance with a common plan.

8. Equal liability of all to labor. Establishment of industrial armies, especially for agriculture.

9. Combination of agriculture with manufacturing industries; gradual abolition of the distinction between town and country, by a more equal distribution of the population over the country.

10. Free education for all children in public schools. Abolition of childrens' factory labor in its present form. Combination of education with industrial production.

Give this some thought while you look closely at the country that we currently live in. In one form or another, all of these components are in place – alive and well in our current Government and politicians. All it needs to push it over the edge is a group of sympathetic law makers and a Commander in Chief to make one sweeping attempt at a power grab while the public ignores the danger. We're here. All they need is for us to sleep one more night while they slowly sneak all the way in......

Liberty and freedom. While provisions are made for them in the Constitution, are not created nor given by it. Those are God given rights. Made by God and not man. Everything on this planet goes as it goes and moves as it does under its own free will. Only mankind can create captivity or oppression of any kind. The denial of these facts is nothing short of denouncing those liberties and God himself.

The U.S. Constitution can only preserve those rights by the people (us) enforcing it and preventing the Government from encroaching upon them.

Meaning? That if we, each of us as an American, do not value our Constitution and uphold it, our Government, through our own apathy as citizens, will erode into a freedom choking, Godless, dehumanizing monster. Our founding fathers and framers of the Constitution knew this. We cannot let it happen.

With that thought in mind, please accept my advice...

Pray. I know some frown upon it, but many, many more glow in that freedom. And, whether you believe in God or not, those who do pray can fight and resist those who salivate at the idea of controlling every aspect of your existence. Those people who may trample you can never have your mind, your soul or your spirit.

Beat on us as a people, crimp our rights down to nothing but bread and water in the days before we face a firing squad and we will still have our prayers to see us through.

So pray. Pray for guidance and wisdom and strength. Pray that God has his will peacefully done. The will of freedom. God has always been a God of choice. You may believe in Him or not. You may pray to Him or not. He has always given you that liberty and freedom. God could have easily created you with built in worship for Him – but he was wise enough to know that the best test of our worthiness is to give us freedom and liberty and see how well we do based on the independent choices that we make.

Pray for that wisdom and pray for it hard – because if we lose our freedoms in this country – we have certainly failed ourselves as a Nation and the good intentions of God.

Be brave. In the upcoming months, patriots will be called names and labeled everything in the book. Ever under the pressure of the Obama administration they are pressing hard against a self appointed timetable to push programs and laws through process that are not wanted or have even been asked for by the American people. I don't know why this urgency exists in their minds, but in doing so, the Office of the President and its' followers are stooping to some low and dangerous tactics.

In the days as I finish this book, I've heard on the news politicians and even the President refer to people, simply speaking their minds as, "The Mob". Insisting that citizens were hired by industry and businesses to protest against their plans and policies.

The White House itself is pushing "PR" trying to retract and put a spin on reliable videos of President Obama flip-flopping on what his true intents are concerning "Single Payer" health care. To add to this they are also asking people to report (whistle blow) on any "fishy" e-mails or BLOG postings made by those who oppose these policies.

We are in terrible dire times.

When our very own government suggests that those who are exercising their 1st amendment right (to their "Freedom of Speech") are somehow "backward", we have a major problem!

What should I make of it when citizens commenting fairly on the undeniable truth are seen as a threat to our Government? What should I think when the White House runs public campaigns against these same good people and their efforts of telling others of that truth? This reeks of communism.

My God what's happening to us?

I'm afraid that we will find that there is more afoot here than meets the eye. The attack on American freedom and liberty is broader than simply two opposing political parties pulling and tugging on policies.

This problem runs deep at a level that is almost un-graspable – but there it is – alive and well.

I'm no conspiracy theorist and there are no black helicopters flying around in my world. But we have a President with no experience, with sketchy friends, partnerships and relations with some very questionable characters and organizations. His campaign? A giant Public Relations machine. His substance? Zero. Experience? Equally zero.

Isn't it funny that everyone assumed that Hillary Clinton was to be the candidate to beat in the Democratic Party for the Presidential run in 2008? What happened to her and her steam?

How did a basic nobody come out of the woodwork and knock the "fair haired lady" of the Democratic Party out of contention? I wonder.

And, before you take lightly in my thoughts that something is nefarious about Mr. Obama sitting in the "big chair", I'd like to remind you of something. We had a successful terrorist attack on this country in 2001 because someone with ill intent studied our "rules" and practices long enough to discover a weakness and exploit it. We should have been paying better attention then and we certainly need to pay better attention today.

Watch everything, and I mean EVERYTHING, closely.

You may as well watch because the truth is... they're watching us.

They are (as I've pointed out in this book) going to take every good thing about us, including our very freedoms and twist them against us – and why? Because it's the only way they can beat us.

They can't turn this country toward socialism, or worse, by following the Constitution. They can't do it in a country where people have the right to free speech, guns, religion or a vote. They certainly can't do their dirty work in a nation where the government is actually run by freedom loving people. They know they first have to diminish those liberties, freedoms and those who support them. Please, put our Constitution first and make it your personal duty to guard and defend it!

Pray, be brave, speak out, don't trust anything unless you can find the facts to back it. When the White House begins running PR campaigns against the truth – you can't trust anything... except the good American people!

Get together in groups and make larger groups. Peacefully speak your mind. Use words like "Sir" and "Ma'am" and be gracious. Don't stoop to anger or violence, false finger pointing or any other foolish tactic.

They are just waiting for some well meaning American to pull out a knife or a gun at a rally or town hall meeting. For that matter, they may even try and incite it or plant one themselves. If that happens, they'll take that one event, use it as an example and try to lock this country down.

Believe me, if they do that and Uncle Sam decides that they need to "disarm" the people for the safety of everyone, all hell will break loose in this nation.

Don't let this happen!!

We don't need to go there. We've never had to in the past. Just act on our Constitution... but do ACT on it.

Assume, as terrible as this sounds, that a trap is being laid for you. When something as simple as the truth can threaten or destroy something, those fearful of the truth will go to great extremes to prevent it from being seen or heard. If you attend a "Tea Party" or a Government Sponsored "Town Hall Meeting" go in a large group. Take video cameras. If that won't do, take a cell phone that records video and somebody keep one rolling at all times.

There have already been some violent incidences at some of these meetings. Eventually, they will force you to leave your cameras and cell phones outside the meeting areas. This will certainly be in the name of "safety and security". Play it smart. Don't go to a meeting where the media isn't invited or doesn't show up. Stay outside and protest and let the world know that you couldn't take your camera inside.

This is not a time to be sitting around on your duff and idly watch things happen! This is a critical time in our history and we will be put to the test as modern patriots. Be peaceful, be factual, be truthful and be involved!

Please teach our children. For the love of all things Holy, teach them.

If you don't know about the founding principles of this nation and the value and importance of liberty – learn! Then teach it to someone else, especially our children. Don't just buy them fireworks on the 4th of July. Find books on the subject of liberty and read to them about it year round. Ask them what they know about key Presidents and key events and help grow their knowledge and appreciation in these matters. Teach them the Pledge of Allegiance and the Star Spangled Banner!

You have to remember that anyone born after about 1975 has no idea what Communism is. They don't remember Korea, Vietnam, the Berlin Wall coming down or the Cold War. They have no working knowledge of what these things were nor any memory of the efforts this country and President Reagan took to keep us away from Communism and to help end it in the U.S.S.R.

They need to know.

They need to understand how fragile this country and our freedoms really are.

To them, our young, what's happening in Washington D.C. is nothing but business as usual. Let them know that it isn't. This is far from how things should be. Teach them.

Keep the faith and stay diligent.

More Americans are lovers of liberty and believers in good strong American values than there are those who don't. Stay positive!

As threatening as the moves from Capitol Hill are these days, please try to keep several things in mind:

First is the Democratically controlled Congress. Add that with a Democratic President and they should have bills and laws being passed to do their bidding constantly... but they aren't.

They are having resistance – both from the American public and from their own party. In short, there are some folks up there who are keeping an anchor thrown out to slow some of this reckless behavior down. Whether it be because of conscious, politics or policy, I don't know or care – but it's a slow down all the same.

Concerning the White House PR machine. While the spin is wrong and completely deceitful (they are clearly lying) – it's a good sign. When the Oval Office has to try and put the attack on the American people, they (politicians) are on the ropes and in deep trouble. Things aren't going good for them when they have to keep trying to "sell" ideas to the public and attempt to vilify good people. These are not the tactics you use when you are running the most powerful country in the world. Glenn Beck said that these tactics were "below" the dignity of the Office of the President, but clearly not below Barack Obama. He's right.

The truth never needs a "spin" and good policy never has to be "sold" to anyone.

Trust your "gut". You know when things are wrong, when they're not exactly right. Take the time to pay closer attention. The current bunch in Washington is expert at "packaging" things by using those "hot topics" that mull around our society and our water coolers.

"Cap and Trade" was masqueraded as a bill to fight "Global Warming". Then it was renamed to reflect the fighting of "Climate Change" when it became obvious that there is no actual data to support global warming. So they just gave it a flexible title that covers everything – no matter what happens with the thermometers around the world.

The lesson from that is this; "Cap and Trade" is not and was never about controlling "global warming" or else they would have dropped the idea and the bill along with the title when they found themselves having to change it. It's about limiting our economy and weakening our financial position – no matter what it's name is.

Same thing with "Universal Healthcare". They've shifted this thing as well. They have put different committees in place, changed the length (as usual) of the bill(s) to include more and more little goodies, all sorts of things, but in the end, nothing unified and substantial.

Think about it, the people didn't bring this thing to their congressmen and ask for someone to create a law. The President mandated this idea and the Washington gang dove all over it. No real research at all into what it would take to do this... what an actual plan would be. The study of the impact on both patients and the economy – nothing. They just pulled out all the items on their "wish lists" and started bolting it together. Placing something as important as ones life and health into the hands of a government is foolish and dangerous.

"Consistent and Crappy"! Think about that when you think about socialized medicine.

Again, always do a gut check on things. Things are rarely as they appear in Washington and here lately, they've been trying to move so fast that they're being very clumsy and careless. Now is a great time to study politicians if you are new at this sort of thing because they are bumbling and stumbling everywhere. Learn this – anything based on liberty and freedom that is Constitutionally founded will never find any objection with the public and will never "stumble". Trust your gut.

Keep your head on a swivel and use your brain! Always follow the money and work things backwards to the source. Quit worrying about what something or someone is going to do for you and your "special interests" and start studying to see who benefits at the top.

Remember, this is your government! Guide it and watch it!

When I first began this book I simply wanted to find a way to get everyone on a same common page and let us unravel our own little issues while we collectively repaired what was wrong with our government.

Throughout the book I think that I've given us all some interesting things to think about and have laid out a very good case for why we should all stick together. How, collectively, we should be aware of the tricks and tactics historically used by Politicians to grow and maintain their ever reaching power over the people.

That hasn't changed, but my urgency is growing after watching the movements of Washington as of late. We have to act fast.

But I beg one thing of you. No matter who you share your understanding with (or maybe your new understanding after having read this book) make sure you have your facts correct and remember that the things that are wrong with this country have happened over time.

There are some who will always believe mindlessly what they're being told. They will instinctively reject whatever it is that you have to say on the subject at hand. Pray for them and keep an open heart and arms toward them.

The goals of our current government are to literally enslave all of us to the machine they're creating. Almost like some twisted Orwellian plot.

Those that believe in this government and their smothering policies and practices are doomed to be trapped in the same snare with all of us if we fail in our efforts to regain our sovereignty and choices as a people.

Even if they don't believe in God or the rights he gave to us all, their human nature will kick in eventually. When they (the blind government believer) are ground down far enough, even they will snap out of it and will look in the mirror that I mentioned in the 1st chapter.

Be there for them. When they see the light, they will feel hurt, dejected and cheated. (Just like you did when you saw the truth.) They are your fellow Americans and, more importantly, they are your fellow man.

Their beliefs, as wrong as they are, are in fact, genuine.

I have very conservative values – but I don't think that people (American Citizens) who are liberals are just evil monsters. Who could blame them for believing the topical "It takes a Village" type of "good" for all of mankind? Their hearts are in the right place, but they aren't using the full power of their reasoning or understanding.

What they haven't figured out is that the politicians have done them a terrible injustice by doing wrong and evil while hiding behind them as a shield and manipulating them. Their genuine needs and their hopes have been used by politicians as nothing more than "vote bait". As beat upon as conservatives may have felt in the past, the truth is that most of us have been wise and skeptical. But the liberal voters...? They have been worked over terribly – and by their "own" people no less..

Many liberals I know spit the names of those like me when we're not looking because we represent those evil "big business" types. Through my personal insistence on fact checking and demanding that people be the masters of their own destinies, I clearly (according to them) have no feelings or compassion toward my fellow man.

If that's true then I guess I have just completed writing one of the longest, heartless "lies" in history.

The core of this book is dedicated to reminding us that "we're all in this together". So despite the fact that our time is running out, be patient with each other and remember that it's not us against, them, them, them and them.

It's us, the American People, everyone against just a single "them".

That "them" is anyone who lies to us or tries to pry freedom out of our hands and use our good intentions, liberty and nature against us.

Make friends and keep friends. Grow your circle. Care for each other and your community. Smile and spread your love. Remember, care and compassion is unavailable in a

Government program. Lend an ear as well as a hand. Many people who trusted "big brother" will soon be shocked and disappointed. Be there for them in the future as you are now for those you already care for. Let no harm come to anyone. Do not let the powers that be divide us further. We are not a mob, we are not troublemakers. We are Americans – all of us, agreeing or not - Red, White and Blue.

Rediscover your passions for liberty. Pray. Learn. Share. Give. Nurture. Teach. Grow. Laugh. Play. Cry. Rest. Fight.

Those are not suggestions. Do a little of each one every day.

I leave you now with my final thought...

I know it hurts. In all that I've said about keeping positive thoughts and giving of ourselves and staying strong, I still know that it hurts.

I can't believe that so much of this is actually happening to my America – and I can't believe that it happened on my watch. It happened in my prime, in my voting and knowledgeable years. Yes, it hurts, and I'm so disappointed in myself. What have I done?

I think about all the young ones today and those that are being born. Will they be coming into a world where their country has a Government that is wrought with corruption and contempt for it's own people and their freedoms?

I feel with a heavy heart that the children of America today will not have a tomorrow where they can use their own natural talents and go as far as they themselves are brave enough to go.

I can't go to the park and watch them playing - and look upon them and all their future dreams - and see them as nothing more than numbers and cattle. Little drones that will line up to go to their government school and see their government doctor, only to go off and let their talents and abilities rot in the government factories and go home to their government allotted children and live in their government assigned housing.

I hate to imagine a group of them sneaking off together after the appointed curfew in a musty basement while the armed government police patrol just outside the door. Huddling there, fighting fear, trembling and silently reading a Bible or a copy of the Constitution that someone has bravely smuggled inside.

Hoping beyond hope that things were different for them.

Just a few short months ago I would have laughed at myself and thanked God that I have such a vivid imagination.

Anymore... I'm not so sure.

Publicly and professionally I may take some ridicule or damage for writing this book. But I'll tell you this, I'll never have it said that in my own way, I didn't try to do something. I had to. Because I love America and it's people. These problems are real and finding a solution matters.

You matter, I matter and the people who don't see it or won't believe it, they matter too.

We can win this and we can adjust this wrong course that we're on. We've got the people and the resources and, at the end of the day, I know that we have the heart, the spirit and the resolve.

We just need to reawaken it.

And trust me, it will come back, everyone will wake up. I just hope and pray that we do it while we're aware of what's going on and not after it's too late.

My prayers, hopes and dreams are with you all.

God Bless You and God Bless America.

~Joey Bruno~

Resources

NOTE

The pages within the Resource section have not been spell checked by a modern American English spell checker.

Because of this you may see unfamiliar spelling or the use of words that were common at the time of the writing of these historical documents.

Rather than modernize the text we have chosen to leave it intact in order to preserve it's authenticity.

Answers to questions from US NATURALIZATION TEST from CHAPTER 2

**AUTHORS NOTE – Here it is, the test answers. Both this information and the questions found in this book were taken directly from the government (www.uscis.gov) website. Every effort has been made to preserve this information pristine, from that site, into this book.

www.uscis.gov

(rev. 01/09)

UPDATED

Civics (History and Government) Questions for the Redesigned (New) Naturalization Test

The 100 civics (history and government) questions and answers for the redesigned (new) naturalization test are listed below. Applicants who filed the Application for Naturalization, Form N-400, on or after October 1, 2008, should study this list. The civics test is an oral test and the USCIS Officer will ask the applicant up to 10 of the 100 civics questions. An applicant must answer 6 out of 10 questions correctly to pass the civics portion of the naturalization test.

Although USCIS is aware that there may be additional correct answers to the 100 civics questions, applicants are encouraged to respond to the civics questions using the answers provided below.

AMERICAN GOVERNMENT

1. *the Constitution*

2. *sets up the government*
   defines the government
   protects basic rights of Americans

3 *We the People*

4   *a change (to the Constitution)*
an addition (to the Constitution)

5.   *the Bill of Rights*

6.   *speech*
religion
assembly
press
petition the government

7.   *twenty-seven (27)*

8.   *announced our independence (from Great Britain)*
declared our independence (from Great Britain)
said that the United States is free (from Great Britain)

9.   *life*
liberty
pursuit of happiness

10.   *You can practice any religion, or not practice a religion.*

11.   *capitalist economy*
market economy

12.   *Everyone must follow the law*
Leaders must obey the law
Government must obey the law
No one is above the law.

B: System of Government

13.   *Congress*
legislative
President
executive
the courts
judicial

14.   *checks and balances*
separation of powers

15.   *the President*

16. *Congress*
Senate and House (of Representatives)
(U.S. or national) legislature

17. *the Senate and House (of Representatives)*

18. *one hundred (100)*

19. *six (6)*

20. • *Answers will vary. [District of Columbia residents and residents of U.S. territories should answer that D.C. (or the territory where the applicant lives) has no U.S. Senators.]*

21. *four hundred thirty-five (435)*

22. *two (2)*

23. *Answers will vary. [Residents of territories with nonvoting Delegates or Resident Commissioners may provide the name of that Delegate or Commissioner. Also acceptable is any statement that the territory has no (voting) Representatives in Congress.]*

24. *all people of the state*

25. *(because of) the state's population*
(because) they have more people
(because) some states have more people

26. *four (4)*

27. *November*

28. *Barack Obama*
Obama

29. *Joseph R. Biden, Jr.*
Joe Biden
Biden

30. *the Vice President*

31. *the Speaker of the House*

32. *the President*

33. *the President*

34. *the President*

35. *advises the President*

36. *Secretary of Agriculture*
Secretary of Commerce
Secretary of Defense
Secretary of Education
Secretary of Energy
Secretary of Health and Human Services
Secretary of Homeland Security
Secretary of Housing and Urban Development
Secretary of the Interior
Secretary of Labor
Secretary of State
Secretary of Transportation
Secretary of the Treasury
Secretary of Veterans Affairs
Attorney General
Vice President

37. *reviews laws*
explains laws
resolves disputes (disagreements)
decides if a law goes against the Constitution

38. *the Supreme Court*

39. *nine (9)*

40. *John Roberts (John G. Roberts, Jr.)*

41. *to print money*
to declare war
to create an army
to make treaties

42. *provide schooling and education*
provide protection (police)
provide safety (fire departments)
give a driver's license
approve zoning and land use

43. *Answers will vary. [District of Columbia residents should answer that D.C. does not have a Governor.]*

44. *Answers will vary. [District of Columbia residents should answer that D.C. is not a state and does not have a capital. Residents of U.S. territories should name the capital of the territory.]*

45. *Democratic and Republican*

46. *Democratic (Party)*

47. *(Nancy) Pelosi*

C: Rights and Responsibilities

48. *Citizens eighteen (18) and older (can vote).*
You don't have to pay (a poll tax) to vote.
Any citizen can vote. (Women and men can vote.)
A male citizen of any race (can vote).

49. *serve on a jury*
vote in a federal election

50. *vote in a federal election*
run for federal office

51. *freedom of expression*
freedom of speech
freedom of assembly
freedom to petition the government
freedom of worship
the right to bear arms

52. *the United States*
the flag

53. *give up loyalty to other countries*
defend the Constitution and laws of the United States
obey the laws of the United States
serve in the U.S. military (if needed)
serve (do important work for) the nation (if needed)
be loyal to the United States

54. *eighteen (18) and older*

55. *vote*
join a political party

help with a campaign
join a civic group
join a community group
give an elected official your opinion on an issue
call Senators and Representatives
publicly support or oppose an issue or policy
run for office
write to a newspaper

56. *April 15*

57. *at age eighteen (18)*
between eighteen (18) and twenty-six (26)

AMERICAN HISTORY

A: Colonial Period and Independence

58. *freedom*
political liberty
religious freedom
economic opportunity
practice their religion
escape persecution

59. *American Indians*
Native Americans

60. *Africans*
people from Africa

61. *because of high taxes (taxation without representation)*
because the British army stayed in their houses (boarding, quartering)
because they didn't have self-government

62. *(Thomas) Jefferson*

63. *July 4, 1776*

64. *New Hampshire*
Massachusetts
Rhode Island
Connecticut
New York
New Jersey

Pennsylvania
Delaware
Maryland
Virginia
North Carolina
South Carolina
Georgia

65. *The Constitution was written*
The Founding Fathers wrote the Constitution.

66. *1787*

67. *(James) Madison*
(Alexander) Hamilton
(John) Jay
Publius

68. *U.S. Diplomat*
oldest member of the Constitutional Convention
first Postmaster General of the United States
writer of "Poor Richard's Almanac"
started the first free libraries

69. *(George) Washington*

70. *(George) Washington*

B: 1800s

71. *the Louisiana Territory*
Louisiana

72. *War of 1812*
Mexican-American War
Civil War
Spanish-American War

73. *the Civil War*
the War between the States

74. *slavery*
economic reasons
states' rights

75. *freed the slaves (Emancipation Proclamation)*
saved (or preserved) the Union
led the United States during the Civil War

76. *freed the slaves*
freed slaves in the Confederacy
freed slaves in the Confederate states
freed slaves in most Southern states

77. *fought for women's rights*
fought for civil rights

C: Recent American History and Other Important Historical Information

78. *World War I*
World War II
Korean War
Vietnam War
(Persian) Gulf War

79. *(Woodrow) Wilson*

80. *(Franklin) Roosevelt*

81. *Japan, Germany, and Italy*

82. *World War II*

83. *Communism*

84. *civil rights (movement)*

85. *fought for civil rights*
worked for equality for all Americans

86. *Terrorists attacked the United States.*

87. *Cherokee*
Navajo
Sioux
Chippewa
Choctaw
Pueblo
Apache
Iroquois
Creek

Blackfeet
Seminole
Cheyenne
Arawak
Shawnee
Mohegan
Huron
Oneida
Lakota
Crow
Teton
Hopi
Inuit

INTEGRATED CIVICS

A: Geography

88. *Missouri (River)*
Mississippi (River)

89. *Pacific (Ocean)*

90. *Atlantic (Ocean)*

91. *Puerto Rico*
U.S. Virgin Islands
American Samoa
Northern Mariana Islands
Guam

92. *Maine*
New Hampshire
Vermont
New York
Pennsylvania
Ohio
Michigan
Minnesota
North Dakota
Montana
Idaho
Washington
Alaska

93. *California*
Arizona
New Mexico
Texas

94. *Washington, D.C.*

95. *New York (Harbor)*
Liberty Island
Also acceptable are New Jersey, near New York City, and on the Hudson (River).

B: Symbols

96. *because there were 13 original colonies*
because the stripes represent the original colonies

97. *because there is one star for each state*
because each star represents a state
because there are 50 states

98. *The Star-Spangled Banner*

C: Holidays

99. *July 4*

100.*New Year's Day*
Martin Luther King, Jr. Day
Presidents' Day
Memorial Day
Independence Day
Labor Day
Columbus Day
Veterans Day
Thanksgiving
Christmas

The Star Spangled Banner

by: Francis Scott Key

Oh! Say can you see by the dawn's early light
What so proudly we hailed at the twilight's last gleaming?
Whose broad stripes and bright stars through the perilous fight,
O'er the ramparts we watched were so gallantly streaming?
And the rockets' red glare, the bombs bursting in air,
Gave proof through the night that our flag was still there.
Oh! say does that star-spangled banner yet wave
O'er the land of the free and the home of the brave?

On the shore, dimly seen through the mists of the deep,
Where the foe's haughty host in dread silence reposes,
What is that which the breeze, o'er the towering steep,
As it fitfully blows, half conceals, half discloses?
Now it catches the gleam of the morning's first beam,
In full glory reflected now shines in the stream:
'Tis the star-spangled banner! Oh long may it wave
O'er the land of the free and the home of the brave.

And where is that band who so vauntingly swore
That the havoc of war and the battle's confusion,
A home and a country should leave us no more!
Their blood has washed out their foul footsteps' pollution.
No refuge could save the hireling and slave
From the terror of flight, or the gloom of the grave:
And the star-spangled banner in triumph doth wave
O'er the land of the free and the home of the brave.

Oh! Thus be it ever, when freemen shall stand
Between their loved home and the war's desolation!
Blessed with victory and peace, may the heav'n rescued land
Praise the Power that hath made and preserved us a nation.
Then conquer we must, when our cause it is just,
And this be our motto: 'In God is our trust.'
And the star-spangled banner in triumph shall wave
O'er the land of the free and the home of the brave!

The Pledge of Allegiance

"I pledge allegiance to the Flag of the United States of America, and to the Republic for which it stands, one Nation under God, indivisible, with liberty and justice for all."

According to the United States Flag Code the pledge should be recited by standing at attention facing the flag with the right hand over the heart. When not in uniform, people should remove any non-religious headdress with their right hand and hold it at the left shoulder, with the right hand being over the heart. People in uniform should remain silent, face the flag, and render the military salute.

The above version of the Pledge of Allegiance is the correct written form of the Pledge. However it usually spoken and taught in broken phrases. While this is incorrect in its' proper punctuation, it is included here for reference:

"I pledge allegiance

to the Flag

of the United States of America

and to the Republic

for which it stands

one Nation

under God

indivisible

with liberty and justice for all."

The Declaration of Independence

Adopted in Congress 4 July 1776

The Unanimous Declaration of the Thirteen United States of America

When, in the course of human events, it becomes necessary for one people to dissolve the political bands which have connected them with another, and to assume among the powers of the earth, the separate and equal station to which the laws of nature and of nature's God entitle them, a decent respect to the opinions of mankind requires that they should declare the causes which impel them to the separation.

We hold these truths to be self-evident, that all men are created equal, that they are endowed by their Creator with certain unalienable rights, that among these are life, liberty and the pursuit of happiness.

That to secure these rights, governments are instituted among men, deriving their just powers from the consent of the governed. That whenever any form of government becomes destructive to these ends, it is the right of the people to alter or to abolish it, and to institute new government, laying its foundation on such principles and organizing its powers in such form, as to them shall seem most likely to effect their safety and happiness.

Prudence, indeed, will dictate that governments long established should not be changed for light and transient causes; and accordingly all experience hath shown that mankind are more disposed to suffer, while evils are sufferable, than to right themselves by abolishing the forms to which they are accustomed. But when a long train of abuses and usurpations, pursuing invariably the same object evinces a design to reduce them under absolute despotism, it is their right, it is their duty, to throw off such government, and to provide new guards for their future security.

Such has been the patient sufferance of these colonies; and such is now the necessity which constrains them to alter their former systems of government. The history of the present King of Great Britain is a history of repeated injuries and usurpations, all having in direct object the establishment of an absolute tyranny over these states. To prove this, let facts be submitted to a candid world.

He has refused his assent to laws, the most wholesome and necessary for the public good.

He has forbidden his governors to pass laws of immediate and pressing importance, unless suspended in their operation till his assent should be obtained; and when so suspended, he has utterly neglected to attend to them.

He has refused to pass other laws for the accommodation of large districts of people, unless those people would relinquish the right of representation in the legislature, a right inestimable to them and formidable to tyrants only.

He has called together legislative bodies at places unusual, uncomfortable, and distant from the depository of their public records, for the sole purpose of fatiguing them into compliance with his measures.

He has dissolved representative houses repeatedly, for opposing with manly firmness his invasions on the rights of the people.

He has refused for a long time, after such dissolutions, to cause others to be elected; whereby the legislative powers, incapable of annihilation, have returned to the people at large for their exercise; the state remaining in the meantime exposed to all the dangers of invasion from without, and convulsions within.

He has endeavored to prevent the population of these states; for that purpose obstructing the laws for naturalization of foreigners; refusing to pass others to encourage their migration hither, and raising the conditions of new appropriations of lands.

He has obstructed the administration of justice, by refusing his assent to laws for establishing judiciary powers.

He has made judges dependent on his will alone, for the tenure of their offices, and the amount and payment of their salaries.

He has erected a multitude of new offices, and sent hither swarms of officers to harass our people, and eat out their substance.

He has kept among us, in times of peace, standing armies without the consent of our legislature. He has affected to render the military independent of and superior to civil power.

He has combined with others to subject us to a jurisdiction foreign to our constitution, and unacknowledged by our laws; giving his assent to their acts of pretended legislation:

For quartering large bodies of armed troops among us:

For protecting them, by mock trial, from punishment for any murders which they should commit on the inhabitants of these states:

For cutting off our trade with all parts of the world:

For imposing taxes on us without our consent:

For depriving us in many cases, of the benefits of trial by jury:

For transporting us beyond seas to be tried for pretended offenses:

For abolishing the free system of English laws in a neighboring province, establishing therein an arbitrary government, and enlarging its boundaries so as to render it at once an example and fit instrument for introducing the same absolute rule in these colonies:

For taking away our charters, abolishing our most valuable laws, and altering fundamentally the forms of our governments:

For suspending our own legislatures, and declaring themselves invested with power to legislate for us in all cases whatsoever.

He has abdicated government here, by declaring us out of his protection and waging war against us.

He has plundered our seas, ravaged our coasts, burned our towns, and destroyed the lives of our people.

He is at this time transporting large armies of foreign mercenaries to complete the works of death, desolation and tyranny, already begun with circumstances of cruelty and perfidy scarcely paralleled in the most barbarous ages, and totally unworthy of the head of a civilized nation.

He has constrained our fellow citizens taken captive on the high seas to bear arms against their country, to become the executioners of their friends and brethren, or to fall themselves by their hands.

He has excited domestic insurrections amongst us, and has endeavored to bring on the inhabitants of our frontiers, the   merciless Indian savages, whose known rule of warfare, is   undistinguished destruction of all ages, sexes and conditions.

In every stage of these oppressions we have petitioned for redress in the most humble terms: our repeated petitions have been answered only by repeated injury. A prince, whose character is thus marked by every act which may define a tyrant, is unfit to be the ruler of a free people.

Nor have we been wanting in attention to our British brethren. We have warned them from time to time of attempts by their legislature to extend an unwarrantable jurisdiction over us. We have reminded them of the circumstances of our emigration and settlement here. We have appealed to their native justice and magnanimity, and we have conjured them by the ties of our common kindred to disavow these usurpations, which, would inevitably interrupt our connections and correspondence. We must, therefore, acquiesce in the necessity, which denounces our separation, and hold them, as we hold the rest of mankind, enemies in war, in peace friends.

We, therefore, the representatives of the United States of America, in General Congress, assembled, appealing to the Supreme Judge of the world for the rectitude of our intentions, do, in the name, and by the authority of the good people of these colonies, solemnly publish and declare, that these united colonies are, and of right ought to be free and independent states; that they are absolved from all allegiance to the British Crown, and that all political connection between them and the state of Great Britain, is and ought to be totally dissolved; and that as free and independent states, they have full power to levey war, conclude peace, contract alliances, establish commerce, and to do all other acts and things which independent states may of right do. And for the support of this declaration, with a firm reliance on the protection of Divine Providence, we mutually pledge to each other our lives, our fortunes and our sacred honor.

Constitution for the United States of America

We the People of the United States, in Order to form a more perfect Union, establish Justice, insure domestic Tranquility, provide for the common defence, promote the general Welfare, and secure the Blessings of Liberty to ourselves and our Posterity, do ordain and establish this Constitution for the United States of America.

Article. I.

[Section 1.] All legislative Powers herein granted shall be vested in a Congress of the United States, which shall consist of a Senate and House of Representatives.

[Section 2.] The House of Representatives shall be composed of Members chosen every second Year by the People of the several States, and the Electors in each State shall have the Qualifications requisite for Electors of the most numerous Branch of the State Legislature.

No Person shall be a Representative who shall not have attained to the Age of twenty five Years, and been seven Years a Citizen of the United States, and who shall not, when elected, be an Inhabitant of that State in which he shall be chosen.

Representatives and direct Taxes shall be apportioned among the several States which may be included within this Union, according to their respective Numbers, which shall be determined by adding to the whole Number of free Persons, including those bound to Service for a Term of Years, and excluding Indians not taxed, three fifths of all other Persons. The actual Enumeration shall be made within three Years after the first Meeting of the Congress of the United States, and within every subsequent Term of ten Years, in such Manner as they shall by Law direct. The Number of Representatives shall not exceed one for every thirty Thousand, but each State shall have at Least one Representative; and until such enumeration shall be made, the State of New Hampshire shall be entitled to chuse three, Massachusetts eight, Rhode-Island and Providence Plantations one, Connecticut five, New-York six, New Jersey four, Pennsylvania eight, Delaware one, Maryland six, Virginia ten, North Carolina five, South Carolina five, and Georgia three.

When vacancies happen in the Representation from any State, the Executive Authority thereof shall issue Writs of Election to fill such Vacancies.

The House of Representatives shall chuse their Speaker and other Officers; and shall have the sole Power of Impeachment.

[Section 3.] The Senate of the United States shall be composed of two Senators from each State, chosen by the Legislature thereof, for six Years; and each Senator shall have one Vote.

Immediately after they shall be assembled in Consequence of the first Election, they shall be divided as equally as may be into three Classes.

The Seats of the Senators of the first Class shall be vacated at the Expiration of the second Year, of the second Class at the Expiration of the fourth Year, and of the third Class at the Expiration of the sixth Year, so that one third may be chosen every second Year; and if Vacancies happen by Resignation, or otherwise, during the Recess of the Legislature of any State, the Executive thereof may make temporary Appointments until the next Meeting of the Legislature, which shall then fill such Vacancies.

No Person shall be a Senator who shall not have attained to the Age of thirty Years, and been nine Years a Citizen of the United States, and who shall not, when elected, be an Inhabitant of that State for which he shall be chosen.

The Vice President of the United States shall be President of the Senate, but shall have no Vote, unless they be equally divided.

The Senate shall chuse their other Officers, and also a President pro tempore, in the Absence of the Vice President, or when he shall exercise the Office of President of the United States.

The Senate shall have the sole Power to try all Impeachments. When sitting for that Purpose, they shall be on Oath or Affirmation. When the President of the United States is tried, the Chief Justice shall preside: And no Person shall be convicted without the Concurrence of two thirds of the Members present.

Judgment in Cases of Impeachment shall not extend further than to removal from Office, and disqualification to hold and enjoy any Office of honor, Trust or Profit under the United States: but the Party convicted shall nevertheless be liable and subject to Indictment, Trial, Judgment and Punishment, according to Law.

[Section 4.] The Times, Places and Manner of holding Elections for Senators and Representatives, shall be prescribed in each State by the Legislature thereof; but the Congress may at any time by Law make or alter such Regulations, except as to the Places of chusing Senators.

The Congress shall assemble at least once in every Year, and such Meeting shall be on the first Monday in December [Modified by Amendment XX], unless they shall by Law appoint a different Day.

[Section 5.] Each House shall be the Judge of the Elections, Returns and Qualifications of its own Members, and a Majority of each shall constitute a Quorum to do Business; but a smaller Number may adjourn from day to day, and may be authorized to compel the Attendance of absent Members, in such Manner, and under such Penalties as each House may provide.

Each House may determine the Rules of its Proceedings, punish its Members for disorderly Behaviour, and, with the Concurrence of two thirds, expel a Member.

Each House shall keep a Journal of its Proceedings, and from time to time publish the same, excepting such Parts as may in their Judgment require Secrecy; and the Yeas and Nays of the Members of either House on any question shall, at the Desire of one fifth of those Present, be entered on the Journal.

Neither House, during the Session of Congress, shall, without the Consent of the other, adjourn for more than three days, nor to any other Place than that in which the two Houses shall be sitting.

[Section 6.] The Senators and Representatives shall receive a Compensation for their Services, to be ascertained by Law, and paid out of the Treasury of the United States. They shall in all Cases, except Treason, Felony and Breach of the Peace, be privileged from Arrest during their Attendance at the Session of their respective Houses, and in going to and returning from the same; and for any Speech or Debate in either House, they shall not be questioned in any other Place.

No Senator or Representative shall, during the Time for which he was elected, be appointed to any civil Office under the Authority of the United States, which shall have been created, or the Emoluments whereof shall have been encreased during such time; and no Person holding any Office under the United States, shall be a Member of either House during his Continuance in Office.

[Section 7.] All Bills for raising Revenue shall originate in the House of Representatives; but the Senate may propose or concur with Amendments as on other Bills.

Every Bill which shall have passed the House of Representatives and the Senate, shall, before it become a Law, be presented to the President of the United States; If he approve he shall sign it, but if not he shall return it, with his Objections to that House in which it shall have originated, who shall enter the Objections at large on their Journal, and proceed to reconsider it. If after such Reconsideration two thirds of that House shall agree to pass the Bill, it shall be sent, together with the Objections, to the other House, by which it shall likewise be reconsidered, and if approved by two thirds of that House, it shall become a Law. But in all such Cases the Votes of both Houses shall be determined by yeas and Nays, and the Names of the Persons voting for and against the Bill shall be entered on the Journal of each House respectively. If any Bill shall not be returned by the President within ten Days (Sundays excepted) after it shall have been presented to him, the Same shall be a Law, in like Manner as if he had signed it, unless the Congress by their Adjournment prevent its Return, in which Case it shall not be a Law.

Every Order, Resolution, or Vote to which the Concurrence of the Senate and House of Representatives may be necessary (except on a question of Adjournment) shall be presented to the President of the United States; and before the Same shall take Effect, shall be approved by him, or being disapproved by him, shall be repassed by two thirds of the Senate and House of Representatives, according to the Rules and Limitations prescribed in the Case of a Bill.

[Section 8.] The Congress shall have Power To lay and collect Taxes, Duties, Imposts and Excises, to pay the Debts and provide for the common Defence and general Welfare of the United States; but all Duties, Imposts and Excises shall be uniform throughout the United States;

To borrow Money on the credit of the United States;

To regulate Commerce with foreign Nations, and among the several States, and with the Indian Tribes;

To establish an uniform Rule of Naturalization, and uniform Laws on the subject of Bankruptcies throughout the United States;

To coin Money, regulate the Value thereof, and of foreign Coin, and fix the Standard of Weights and Measures;

To provide for the Punishment of counterfeiting the Securities and current Coin of the United States;

To establish Post Offices and post Roads;

To promote the Progress of Science and useful Arts, by securing for limited Times to Authors and Inventors the exclusive Right to their respective Writings and Discoveries;

To constitute Tribunals inferior to the supreme Court;

To define and punish Piracies and Felonies committed on the high Seas, and Offences against the Law of Nations;

To declare War, grant Letters of Marque and Reprisal, and make Rules concerning Captures on Land and Water;

To raise and support Armies, but no Appropriation of Money to that Use shall be for a longer Term than two Years;

To provide and maintain a Navy;

To make Rules for the Government and Regulation of the land and naval Forces;

To provide for calling forth the Militia to execute the Laws of the Union, suppress Insurrections and repel Invasions;

To provide for organizing, arming, and disciplining, the Militia, and for governing such Part of them as may be employed in the Service of the United States, reserving to the States respectively, the Appointment of the Officers, and the Authority of training the Militia according to the discipline prescribed by Congress;

To exercise exclusive Legislation in all Cases whatsoever, over such District (not exceeding ten Miles square) as may, by Cession of particular States, and the Acceptance of Congress, become the Seat of the Government of the United States, and to exercise like Authority over all Places purchased by the Consent of the Legislature of the State in which the Same shall be, for the Erection of Forts, Magazines, Arsenals, dock-Yards, and other needful Buildings; --And To make all Laws which shall be necessary and proper for carrying into Execution the foregoing Powers, and all other Powers vested by this Constitution in the Government of the United States, or in any Department or Officer thereof.

[Section 9.] The Migration or Importation of such Persons as any of the States now existing shall think proper to admit, shall not be prohibited by the Congress prior to the Year one thousand eight hundred and eight, but a Tax or duty may be imposed on such Importation, not exceeding ten dollars for each Person.

The Privilege of the Writ of Habeas Corpus shall not be suspended, unless when in Cases of Rebellion or Invasion the public Safety may require it.

No Bill of Attainder or ex post facto Law shall be passed.

No Capitation, or other direct, Tax shall be laid, unless in Proportion to the Census or Enumeration herein before directed to be taken.

No Tax or Duty shall be laid on Articles exported from any State.

No Preference shall be given by any Regulation of Commerce or Revenue to the Ports of one State over those of another; nor shall Vessels bound to, or from, one State, be obliged to enter, clear, or pay Duties in another.

No Money shall be drawn from the Treasury, but in Consequence of Appropriations made by Law; and a regular Statement and Account of the Receipts and Expenditures of all public Money shall be published from time to time.

No Title of Nobility shall be granted by the United States: And no Person holding any Office of Profit or Trust under them, shall, without the Consent of the Congress, accept of any present, Emolument, Office, or Title, of any kind whatever, from any King, Prince, or foreign State.

[Section 10.] No State shall enter into any Treaty, Alliance, or Confederation; grant Letters of Marque and Reprisal; coin Money; emit Bills of Credit; make any Thing but gold and silver Coin a Tender in Payment of Debts; pass any Bill of Attainder, ex post facto Law, or Law impairing the Obligation of Contracts, or grant any Title of Nobility.

No State shall, without the Consent of the Congress, lay any Imposts or Duties on Imports or Exports, except what may be absolutely necessary for executing it's inspection Laws; and the net Produce of all Duties and Imposts, laid by any State on Imports or Exports, shall be for the Use of the Treasury of the United States; and all such Laws shall be subject to the Revision and Controul of the Congress.

No State shall, without the Consent of Congress, lay any Duty of Tonnage, keep Troops, or Ships of War in time of Peace, enter into any Agreement or Compact with another State, or with a foreign Power, or engage in War, unless actually invaded, or in such imminent Danger as will not admit of delay.

Article. II.

[Section 1.] The executive Power shall be vested in a President of the United States of America. He shall hold his Office during the Term of four Years, and, together with the Vice President, chosen for the same Term, be elected, as follows:

Each State shall appoint, in such Manner as the Legislature thereof may direct, a Number of Electors, equal to the whole Number of Senators and Representatives to which the State may be entitled in the Congress: but no Senator or Representative, or Person holding an Office of Trust or Profit under the United States, shall be appointed an Elector.

The Electors shall meet in their respective States, and vote by Ballot for two Persons, of whom one at least shall not be an Inhabitant of the same State with themselves. And they shall make a List of all the Persons voted for, and of the Number of Votes for each; which List they shall sign and certify, and transmit sealed to the Seat of the Government of the United States, directed to the President of the Senate. The President of the Senate shall, in the Presence of the Senate and House of Representatives, open all the Certificates, and the Votes shall then be counted. The Person having the greatest Number of Votes shall be the President, if such Number be a Majority of the whole Number of Electors appointed; and if there be more than one who have such Majority, and have an equal Number of Votes, then the House of Representatives shall immediately chuse by Ballot one of them for President; and if no Person have a Majority, then from the five highest on the List the said House shall in like Manner chuse the President. But in chusing the President, the Votes shall be taken by States, the Representation from each State having one Vote; a quorum for this Purpose shall consist of a Member or Members from two thirds of the States, and a Majority of all the States shall be necessary to a Choice. In every Case, after the Choice of the President, the Person having the greatest Number of Votes of the Electors shall be the Vice President. But if there should remain two or more who have equal Votes, the Senate shall chuse from them by Ballot the Vice President.

The Congress may determine the Time of chusing the Electors, and the Day on which they shall give their Votes; which Day shall be the same throughout the United States.

No Person except a natural born Citizen, or a Citizen of the United States, at the time of the Adoption of this Constitution, shall be eligible to the Office of President; neither shall any Person be eligible to that Office who shall not have attained to the Age of thirty five Years, and been fourteen Years a Resident within the United States.

In Case of the Removal of the President from Office, or of his Death, Resignation, or Inability to discharge the Powers and Duties of the said Office, the Same shall devolve on the Vice President, and the Congress may by Law provide for the Case of Removal, Death, Resignation or Inability, both of the President and Vice President, declaring what Officer shall then act as President, and such Officer shall act accordingly, until the Disability be removed, or a President shall be elected.

The President shall, at stated Times, receive for his Services, a Compensation, which shall neither be increased nor diminished during the Period for which he shall have been elected, and he shall not receive within that Period any other Emolument from the United States, or any of them.

Before he enter on the Execution of his Office, he shall take the following Oath or Affirmation: -- *"I do solemnly swear (or affirm) that I will faithfully execute the Office of President of the United States, and will to the best of my Ability, preserve, protect and defend the Constitution of the United States."*

[Section 2.] The President shall be Commander in Chief of the Army and Navy of the United States, and of the Militia of the several States, when called into the actual Service of the United States; he may require the Opinion, in writing, of the principal Officer in each of the executive Departments, upon any Subject relating to the Duties of their respective Offices, and he shall have Power to grant Reprieves and Pardons for Offences against the United States, except in Cases of Impeachment.

He shall have Power, by and with the Advice and Consent of the Senate, to make Treaties, provided two thirds of the Senators present concur; and he shall nominate, and by and with the Advice and Consent of the Senate, shall appoint Ambassadors, other public Ministers and Consuls, Judges of the supreme Court, and all other Officers of the United States, whose Appointments are not herein otherwise provided for, and which shall be established by Law: but the Congress may by Law vest the Appointment of such inferior Officers, as they think proper, in the President alone, in the Courts of Law, or in the Heads of Departments.

The President shall have Power to fill up all Vacancies that may happen during the Recess of the Senate, by granting Commissions which shall expire at the End of their next Session.

[Section 3.] He shall from time to time give to the Congress Information of the State of the Union, and recommend to their Consideration such Measures as he shall judge necessary and expedient; he may, on extraordinary Occasions, convene both Houses, or either of them, and in Case of Disagreement between them, with Respect to the Time of Adjournment, he may adjourn them to such Time as he shall think proper; he shall receive Ambassadors and other public Ministers; he shall take Care that the Laws be faithfully executed, and shall Commission all the Officers of the United States.

[Section 4.] The President, Vice President and all civil Officers of the United States, shall be removed from Office on Impeachment for, and Conviction of, Treason, Bribery, or other high Crimes and Misdemeanors.

Article. III.

[Section 1.] The judicial Power of the United States shall be vested in one supreme Court, and in such inferior Courts as the Congress may from time to time ordain and establish. The Judges, both of the supreme and inferior Courts, shall hold their Offices during good Behaviour, and shall, at stated Times, receive for their Services a Compensation, which shall not be diminished during their Continuance in Office.

[Section 2.] The judicial Power shall extend to all Cases, in Law and Equity, arising under this Constitution, the Laws of the United States, and

Treaties made, or which shall be made, under their Authority; -- to all Cases affecting Ambassadors, other public Ministers and Consuls; -- to all Cases of admiralty and maritime Jurisdiction; -- to Controversies to which the United States shall be a Party; -- to Controversies between two or more States; -- between a State and Citizens of another State; -- between Citizens of different States; -- between Citizens of the same State claiming Lands under Grants of different States, and between a State, or the Citizens thereof, and foreign States, Citizens or Subjects.

In all Cases affecting Ambassadors, other public Ministers and Consuls, and those in which a State shall be Party, the supreme Court shall have original Jurisdiction. In all the other Cases before mentioned, the supreme Court shall have appellate Jurisdiction, both as to Law and Fact, with such Exceptions, and under such Regulations as the Congress shall make.

The Trial of all Crimes, except in Cases of Impeachment, shall be by Jury; and such Trial shall be held in the State where the said Crimes shall have been committed; but when not committed within any State, the Trial shall be at such Place or Places as the Congress may by Law have directed.

[Section 3.] Treason against the United States shall consist only in levying War against them, or in adhering to their Enemies, giving them Aid and Comfort. No Person shall be convicted of Treason unless on the Testimony of two Witnesses to the same overt Act, or on Confession in open Court.

The Congress shall have Power to declare the Punishment of Treason, but no Attainder of Treason shall work Corruption of Blood, or Forfeiture except during the Life of the Person attainted.

Article. IV.

[Section 1.] Full Faith and Credit shall be given in each State to the public Acts, Records, and judicial Proceedings of every other State. And the Congress may by general Laws prescribe the Manner in which such Acts, Records and Proceedings shall be proved, and the Effect thereof.

[Section 2.] The Citizens of each State shall be entitled to all Privileges and Immunities of Citizens in the several States.

A Person charged in any State with Treason, Felony, or other Crime, who shall flee from Justice, and be found in another State, shall on Demand of the executive Authority of the State from which he fled, be delivered up, to be removed to the State having Jurisdiction of the Crime.

No Person held to Service or Labour in one State, under the Laws thereof, escaping into another, shall, in Consequence of any Law or Regulation therein, be discharged from such Service or Labour, but shall be delivered up on Claim of the Party to whom such Service or Labour may be due.

[Section 3.] New States may be admitted by the Congress into this Union; but no new State shall be formed or erected within the Jurisdiction of any other State; nor any State be formed by the Junction of two or more States, or Parts of States, without the Consent of the Legislatures of the States concerned as well as of the Congress.

The Congress shall have Power to dispose of and make all needful Rules and Regulations respecting the Territory or other Property belonging to the United States; and nothing in this Constitution shall be so construed as to Prejudice any Claims of the United States, or of any particular State.

[Section 4.] The United States shall guarantee to every State in this Union a Republican Form of Government, and shall protect each of them against Invasion; and on Application of the Legislature, or of the Executive (when the Legislature cannot be convened), against domestic Violence.

Article. V.

The Congress, whenever two thirds of both Houses shall deem it necessary, shall propose Amendments to this Constitution, or, on the Application of the Legislatures of two thirds of the several States, shall call a Convention for proposing Amendments, which, in either Case, shall be valid to all Intents and Purposes, as Part of this Constitution, when ratified by the Legislatures of three fourths of the several States, or by Conventions in three fourths thereof, as the one or the other Mode of Ratification may be proposed by the Congress; Provided that no Amendment which may be made prior to the Year One thousand eight hundred and eight shall in any Manner affect the first and fourth Clauses in the Ninth Section of the first Article; and that no State, without its Consent, shall be deprived of its equal Suffrage in the Senate.

Article. VI.

All Debts contracted and Engagements entered into, before the Adoption of this Constitution, shall be as valid against the United States under this Constitution, as under the Confederation.

This Constitution, and the Laws of the United States which shall be made in Pursuance thereof; and all Treaties made, or which shall be made, under the Authority of the United States, shall be the supreme Law of the Land; and the Judges in every State shall be bound thereby, any Thing in the Constitution or Laws of any State to the Contrary notwithstanding.

The Senators and Representatives before mentioned, and the Members of the several State Legislatures, and all executive and judicial Officers, both of the United States and of the several States, shall be bound by Oath or

Affirmation, to support this Constitution; but no religious Test shall ever be required as a Qualification to any Office or public Trust under the United States.

Article. VII.

The Ratification of the Conventions of nine States, shall be sufficient for the Establishment of this Constitution between the States so ratifying the Same.

Done in Convention by the Unanimous Consent of the States present the Seventeenth Day of September in the Year of our Lord one thousand seven hundred and Eighty seven and of the Independence of the United States of America the Twelfth In witness whereof We have hereunto subscribed our Names,

Go. Washington	Presidt. and deputy from Virginia
New Hampshire	*John Langdon, Nicholas Gilman*
Massachusetts	*Nathaniel Gorham, Rufus King*
Connecticut	*Wm. Saml. Johnson, Roger Sherman*
New York	*Alexander Hamilton*
New Jersey	*Wil: Livingston, David Brearley, Wm. Paterson, Jona: Dayton*
Pennsylvania	*B. Franklin, Thomas Mifflin, Robt Morris*
	Geo. Clymer, Thos. Fitz Simons, Jared Ingersoll, James Wilson, Gouv Morris
Delaware	*Geo: Read, Gunning Bedford jun, John Dickinson, Richard Bassett, Jaco: Broom*
Maryland	*James Mchenry, Dan of St Thos. Jenifer, Danl Carroll*
Virginia	*John Blair, James Madison*
North Carolina	*Wm. Blount, Richd. Dobbs Spaight, Hu Williamson*
South Carolina	*J. Rutledge, Charles Cotesworth Pinckney*
	Charles Pinckney, Pierce Butler
Georgia	*William Few, Abr Baldwin*

In Convention Monday, September 17th, 1787.
Present
The States of

New Hampshire, Massachusetts, Connecticut, Mr. Hamilton from New York, New Jersey, Pennsylvania, Delaware, Maryland, Virginia, North Carolina, South Carolina and Georgia.

Resolved,

That the preceeding Constitution be laid before the United States in Congress assembled, and that it is the Opinion of this Convention, that it should afterwards be submitted to a Convention of Delegates, chosen in each State by the People thereof, under the Recommendation of its Legislature, for their Assent and Ratification; and that each Convention assenting to, and ratifying the Same, should give Notice thereof to the United States in Congress assembled. Resolved, That it is the Opinion of this Convention, that as soon as the Conventions of nine States shall have ratified this Constitution, the United States in Congress assembled should fix a Day on which Electors should be appointed by the States which have ratified the same, and a Day on which the Electors should assemble to vote for the President, and the Time and Place for commencing Proceedings under this Constitution. That after such Publication the Electors should be appointed, and the Senators and Representatives elected: That the Electors should meet on the Day fixed for the Election of the President, and should transmit their Votes certified, signed, sealed and directed, as the Constitution requires, to the Secretary of the United States in Congress assembled, that the Senators and Representatives should convene at the Time and Place assigned; that the Senators should appoint a President of the Senate, for the sole purpose of receiving, opening and counting the Votes for President; and, that after he shall be chosen, the Congress, together with the President, should, without Delay, proceed to execute this Constitution.

By the Unanimous Order of the Convention

Go. Washington--Presidt.

W. Jackson Secretary.

Bill of Rights

The conventions of a number of the States having at the time of their adopting the Constitution, expressed a desire, in order to prevent misconstruction or abuse of its powers, that further declaratory and restrictive clauses should be added.

Article the first [Not Ratified]

After the first enumeration required by the first article of the Constitution, there shall be one Representative for every thirty thousand, until the number shall amount to one hundred, after which the proportion shall be so regulated by Congress, that there shall be not less than one hundred Representatives, nor less than one Representative for every forty thousand persons, until the number of Representatives shall amount to two hundred; after which the proportion shall be so regulated by Congress, that there shall not be less than two hundred Representatives, nor more than one Representative for every fifty thousand persons.

Article the second [Amendment XXVII - Ratified 1992]

No law, varying the compensation for the services of the Senators and Representatives, shall take effect, until an election of Representatives shall have intervened.

Article the third [Amendment I]

Congress shall make no law respecting an establishment of religion, or prohibiting the free exercise thereof; or abridging the freedom of speech, or of the press; or the right of the people peaceably to assemble, and to petition the Government for a redress of grievances.

Article the fourth [Amendment II]

A well regulated Militia, being necessary to the security of a free State, the right of the people to keep and bear Arms, shall not be infringed.

Article the fifth [Amendment III]

No Soldier shall, in time of peace be quartered in any house, without the consent of the Owner, nor in time of war, but in a manner to be prescribed by law.

Article the sixth [Amendment IV]

The right of the people to be secure in their persons, houses, papers, and effects, against unreasonable searches and seizures, shall not be violated, and no Warrants shall issue, but upon probable cause, supported by Oath or affirmation, and particularly describing the place to be searched, and the persons or things to be seized.

Article the seventh [Amendment V]

No person shall be held to answer for a capital, or otherwise infamous crime, unless on a presentment or indictment of a Grand Jury, except in cases arising in the land or naval forces, or in the Militia, when in actual service in time of War or public danger; nor shall any person be subject for the same offence to be twice put in jeopardy of life or limb; nor shall be compelled in any criminal case to be a witness against himself, nor be deprived of life, liberty, or property, without due process of law; nor shall private property be taken for public use, without just compensation.

Article the eighth [**Amendment VI**]

In all criminal prosecutions, the accused shall enjoy the right to a speedy and public trial, by an impartial jury of the State and district wherein the crime shall have been committed, which district shall have been previously ascertained by law, and to be informed of the nature and cause of the accusation; to be confronted with the witnesses against him; to have compulsory process for obtaining witnesses in his favor, and to have the Assistance of Counsel for his defence.

Article the ninth [**Amendment VII**]

In Suits at common law, where the value in controversy shall   exceed twenty dollars, the right of trial by jury shall be preserved, and no fact tried by a jury, shall be otherwise re-examined in any Court of the United States, than according to the rules of the common law.

Article the tenth [**Amendment VIII**]

Excessive bail shall not be required, nor excessive fines imposed, nor cruel and unusual punishments inflicted.

Article the eleventh [**Amendment IX**]

The enumeration in the Constitution, of certain rights, shall not be construed to deny or disparage others retained by the people.

Article the twelfth [**Amendment X**]

The powers not delegated to the United States by the Constitution, nor prohibited by it to the States, are reserved to the States respectively, or to the people.

Additional Amendments to the Constitution

ARTICLES in addition to, and Amendment of, the Constitution of the United States of America, proposed by Congress, and ratified by the Legislatures of the several States, pursuant to the fifth Article of the original Constitution

Article XI

[Proposed 1794; Ratified 1798]

The Judicial power of the United States shall not be construed to extend to any suit in law or equity, commenced or prosecuted against one of the United States by Citizens of another State, or by Citizens or Subjects of any Foreign State.

Article XII

[Proposed 1803; Ratified 1804]

The Electors shall meet in their respective states, and vote by ballot for President and Vice-President, one of whom, at least, shall not be an inhabitant of the same state with themselves; they shall name in their ballots the person voted for as President, and in distinct ballots the person voted for as Vice-President, and they shall make distinct lists of all persons voted for as President, and of all persons voted for as Vice-President, and of the number of votes for each, which lists they shall sign and certify, and transmit sealed to the seat of the government of the United States, directed to the President of the Senate;-- The President of the Senate shall, in the presence of the Senate and House of Representatives, open all the certificates and the votes shall then be counted;--The person having the greatest number of votes for President, shall be the President, if such number be a majority of the whole number of Electors appointed; and if no person have such majority, then from the persons having the highest numbers not exceeding three on the list of those voted for as President, the House of Representatives shall choose immediately, by ballot, the President. But in choosing the President, the votes shall be taken by states, the representation from each state having one vote; a quorum for this purpose shall consist of a member or members from two-thirds of the states, and a majority of all the states shall be necessary to a choice. And if the House of Representatives shall not choose a President whenever the right of choice shall devolve upon them, before the fourth day of March next following, then the Vice-President shall act as President, as in the case of the death or other constitutional disability of the President.-- The person having the greatest number of votes as Vice-President, shall be the Vice-President, if such number be a majority of the whole number of Electors appointed, and if no person have a majority, then from the two highest numbers on the list, the Senate shall choose the Vice-President; a quorum for the purpose shall consist of two-thirds of the whole number of Senators, and a majority of the whole number shall be necessary to a choice. But no person constitutionally ineligible to the office of President shall be eligible to that of Vice-President of the United States.

[Contested Article.]

[Proposed 1810; Probably Ratified 1819]

If any Citizen of the United States shall accept, claim, receive or retain any Title of Nobility or Honour, or shall, without the Consent of Congress, accept and retain any present, Pension, Office or Emolument of any kind whatever, from any Emperor, King, Prince or foreign Power, such Person shall cease to be a Citizen of the United States, and shall be incapable of holding any Office of Trust or Profit under them, or either of them.

[Unratified Article.]

[Proposed 1861; Endorsed by President-elect Lincoln; Unratified]

Article Thirteen.

No amendment shall be made to the Constitution which will authorize or give to Congress the power to abolish or interfere, within any State, with the domestic institutions thereof, including that of persons held to labor or service by the laws of said State.

Article. XIII.

[Proposed 1865; Ratified 1865]

Section. 1. Neither slavery nor involuntary servitude, except as a punishment for crime whereof the party shall have been duly convicted, shall exist within the United States, or any place subject to their jurisdiction.

Section. 2. Congress shall have power to enforce this article by appropriate legislation.

Article. XIV.

[Proposed 1866; Ratified Under Duress 1868]

Section. 1. All persons born or naturalized in the United States, and subject to the jurisdiction thereof, are citizens of the United States and of the State wherein they reside. No State shall make or enforce any law which shall abridge the privileges or immunities of citizens of the United States; nor shall any State deprive any person of life, liberty, or property, without due process of law; nor deny to any person within its jurisdiction the equal protection of the laws.

Section. 2. Representatives shall be apportioned among the several States according to their respective numbers, counting the whole number of persons in each State, excluding Indians not taxed. But when the right to vote at any election for the choice of electors for President and Vice President of the United States, Representatives in Congress, the Executive and Judicial officers of a State, or the members of the Legislature thereof, is denied to any of the male inhabitants of such State, being twenty-one years of age, and citizens of the United States, or in any way abridged, except for participation in rebellion, or other crime, the basis of representation therein shall be reduced in the proportion which the number of such male citizens shall bear to the whole number of male citizens twenty-one years of age in such State.

Section. 3. No person shall be a Senator or Representative in Congress, or elector of President and Vice President, or hold any office, civil or military, under the United States, or under any State, who, having previously taken an oath, as a member of Congress, or as an officer of the United States, or as a member of any State legislature, or as an executive or judicial officer of any State, to support the Constitution of the United States, shall have engaged in insurrection or rebellion against the same, or given aid or comfort to the enemies thereof. But Congress may by a vote of two-thirds of each House, remove such disability.

Section. 4. The validity of the public debt of the United States, authorized by law, including debts incurred for payment of pensions and bounties for services in suppressing insurrection or rebellion, shall not be questioned. But neither the United States nor any State shall assume or pay any debt or obligation incurred in aid of insurrection or rebellion against the United States, or any claim for the loss or emancipation of any slave; but all such debts, obligations and claims shall be held illegal and void.

Section. 5. The Congress shall have power to enforce, by appropriate legislation, the provisions of this article.

Article. XV.
[Proposed 1869; Ratified 1870]

Section. 1. The right of citizens of the United States to vote shall not be denied or abridged by the United States or by any State on account of race, color, or previous condition of servitude.

Section. 2. The Congress shall have power to enforce this article by appropriate legislation.

Article XVI
[Proposed 1909; Questionably Ratified 1913]

The Congress shall have power to lay and collect taxes on incomes, from whatever source derived, without apportionment among the several States, and without regard to any census or enumeration.

Article XVII
[Proposed 1912; Ratified 1913]

The Senate of the United States shall be composed of two Senators from each State, elected by the people thereof, for six years; and each Senator shall have one vote. The electors in each State shall have the qualifications requisite for electors of the most numerous branch of the State legislatures.

When vacancies happen in the representation of any State in the Senate, the executive authority of such State shall issue writs of election to fill such vacancies: Provided, That the legislature of any State may empower the executive thereof to make temporary appointments until the people fill the vacancies by election as the legislature may direct.

This amendment shall not be so construed as to affect the election or term of any Senator chosen before it becomes valid as part of the Constitution.

Article XVIII

[Proposed 1917; Ratified 1919; Repealed 1933 (See Amendment XXI, Section 1]

Section. 1. After one year from the ratification of this article the manufacture, sale, or transportation of intoxicating liquors within, the importation thereof into, or the exportation thereof from the United States and all territory subject to the jurisdiction thereof for beverage purposes is hereby prohibited.

Section. 2. The Congress and the several States shall have concurrent power to enforce this article by appropriate legislation.

Section. 3. This article shall be inoperative unless it shall have been ratified as an amendment to the Constitution by the legislatures of the several States, as provided in the Constitution, within seven years from the date of the submission hereof to the States by the Congress.

Article XIX

[Proposed 1919; Ratified 1920]

The right of citizens of the United States to vote shall not be denied or abridged by the United States or by any State on account of sex. Congress shall have power to enforce this article by appropriate legislation.

[Unratified Article.]

[Proposed 1926; Unratified]

Article-- Section. 1. The Congress shall have power to limit, regulate, and prohibit the labor of persons under eighteen years of age.

Section. 2. The power of the several States is unimpaired by this article except that the operation of State laws shall be suspended to the extent necessary to give effect to legislation enacted by the Congress.

Article XX

[Proposed 1932; Ratified 1933]

Section. 1. The terms of the President and Vice President shall end at noon on the 20th day of January, and the terms of Senators and Representatives at noon on the 3d day of January, of the years in which such terms would have ended if this article had not been ratified; and the terms of their successors shall then begin.

Section. 2. The Congress shall assemble at least once in every year, and such meeting shall begin at noon on the 3d day of January, unless they shall by law appoint a different day.

Section. 3. If, at the time fixed for the beginning of the term of the President, the President elect shall have died, the Vice President elect shall become President. If a President shall not have been chosen before the time fixed for the beginning of his term, or if the President elect shall have failed to qualify, then the Vice President elect shall act as President until a President shall have qualified; and the Congress may by law provide for the case wherein neither a President elect nor a Vice President elect shall have qualified, declaring who shall then act as President, or the manner in which one who is to act shall be selected, and such person shall act accordingly until a President or Vice President shall have qualified.

Section. 4. The Congress may by law provide for the case of the death of any of the persons from whom the House of Representatives may choose a President whenever the right of choice shall have devolved upon them, and for the case of the death of any of the persons from whom the Senate may choose a Vice President whenever the right of choice shall have devolved upon them.

Section. 5. Sections 1 and 2 shall take effect on the 15th day of October following the ratification of this article.

Section. 6. This article shall be inoperative unless it shall have been ratified as an amendment to the Constitution by the legislatures of three-fourths of the several States within seven years from the date of its submission.

Article. XXI

[Proposed 1933; Ratified 1933]

Section. 1. The eighteenth article of amendment to the Constitution of the United States is hereby repealed.

Section. 2. The transportation or importation into any State, Territory, or possession of the United States for delivery or use therein of intoxicating liquors, in violation of the laws thereof, is hereby prohibited.

Section. 3. This article shall be inoperative unless it shall have been ratified as an amendment to the Constitution by conventions in the several States, as provided in the Constitution, within seven years from the date of the submission hereof to the States by the Congress.

Article XXII

[Proposed 1947; Ratified 1951]

Section. 1. No person shall be elected to the office of the President more than twice, and no person who has held the office of President, or acted as President, for more than two years of a term to which some other person was elected President shall be elected to the office of the President more than once. But this Article shall not apply to any person holding the office of President when this Article was proposed by the Congress, and shall not prevent any person who may be holding the office of President, or acting as President, during the term within which this Article becomes operative from holding the office of President or acting as President during the remainder of such term.

Section. 2. This article shall be inoperative unless it shall have been ratified as an amendment to the Constitution by the legislatures of three-fourths of the several States within seven years from the date of its submission to the States by the Congress.

Article XXIII

[Proposed 1960; Ratified 1961]

Section. 1. The District constituting the seat of Government of the United States shall appoint in such manner as the Congress may direct: A number of electors of President and Vice President equal to the whole number of Senators and Representatives in Congress to which the District would be entitled if it were a State, but in no event more than the least populous State; they shall be in addition to those appointed by the States, but they shall be considered, for the purposes of the election of President and Vice President, to be electors appointed by a State; and they shall meet in the District and perform such duties as provided by the twelfth article of amendment.

Section. 2. The Congress shall have power to enforce this article by appropriate legislation.

Article XXIV

[Proposed 1962; Ratified 1964]

Section. 1. The right of citizens of the United States to vote in any primary or other election for President or Vice President, for electors for President or Vice President, or for Senator or Representative in Congress, shall not be denied or abridged by the United States or any

State by reason of failure to pay any poll tax or other tax.

Section. 2. The Congress shall have power to enforce this article by appropriate legislation.

Article XXV

Section. 1. In case of the removal of the President from office or of his death or resignation, the Vice President shall become President.

Section. 2. Whenever there is a vacancy in the office of the Vice President, the President shall nominate a Vice President who shall take office upon confirmation by a majority vote of both Houses of Congress.

Section. 3. Whenever the President transmits to the President pro tempore of the Senate and the Speaker of the House of Representatives his written declaration that he is unable to discharge the powers and duties of his office, and until he transmits to them a written declaration to the contrary, such powers and duties shall be discharged by the Vice President as Acting President.

Section. 4. Whenever the Vice President and a majority of either the principal officers of the executive departments or of such other body as Congress may by law provide, transmit to the President pro tempore of the Senate and the Speaker of the House of Representatives their written declaration that the President is unable to discharge the powers and duties of his office, the Vice President shall immediately assume the powers and duties of the office as Acting President. Thereafter, when the President transmits to the President pro tempore of the Senate and the Speaker of the House of Representatives his written declaration that no inability exists, he shall resume the powers and duties of his office unless the Vice President and a majority of either the principal officers of the executive department or of such other body as Congress may by law provide, transmit within four days to the President pro tempore of the Senate and the Speaker of the House of Representatives their written declaration that the President is unable to discharge the powers and duties of his office. Thereupon Congress shall decide the issue, assembling within forty-eight hours for that purpose if not in session. If the Congress, within twenty-one days after receipt of the latter written declaration, or, if Congress is not in session, within twenty-one days after Congress is required to assemble, determines by two-thirds vote of both Houses that the President is unable to discharge the powers and duties of his office, the Vice President shall continue to discharge the same as Acting President; otherwise, the President shall resume the powers and duties of his office.

Article XXVI

[Proposed 1971; Ratified 1971]

Section. 1. The right of citizens of the United States, who are eighteen years of age or older, to vote shall not be denied or abridged by the United States or by any State on account of age.

Section. 2. The Congress shall have power to enforce this article by appropriate legislation.

[Inoperative Article.]

[Proposed 1972; Expired Unratified 1982]

Article-- Section. 1. Equality of rights under the law shall not be denied or abridged by the United States or by any State on account of sex.

Section. 2. The Congress shall have the power to enforce, by appropriate legislation, the provisions of this article.

Section. 3. This amendment shall take effect two years after the date of ratification.

[Proposed 1978; Expired Unratified 1985]

Article-- Section. 1. For purposes of representation in the Congress, election of the President and Vice President, and article V of this Constitution, the District constituting the seat of government of the United States shall be treated as though it were a State.

Section. 2. The exercise of the rights and powers conferred under this article shall be by the people of the District constituting the seat of government, and as shall be provided by the Congress.

Section. 3. The twenty-third article of amendment to the Constitution of the United States is hereby repealed.

Section. 4. This article shall be inoperative, unless it shall have been ratified as an amendment to the Constitution by the legislatures of three-fourths of the several States within seven years from the date of its submission.

Article XXVII

[Proposed 1789; Ratified 1992; Second of twelve Articles comprising the Bill of Rights]

No law, varying the compensation for the services of the Senators and Representatives, shall take effect, until an election of Representatives shall have intervened.

Contacts and Info

Joey Bruno - For speaking engagements, interviews and other information, please contact him through:

www.modernpatriots.com

joey@modernpatriots.com

"We The People" The Show – Started as a dovetail project with the "Modern Patriot" series; "We The People" is a one man show hosted by Joey Bruno. This production is a stirring experience for the whole family and, like his writings, is for Americans of all ages, races, religions and party affiliations.

Typeface, book information and other goodies of interest to the writer crowd:

Divided we Fall is set in the "Garamond" font. It was chosen for its' friendly and casual appearance as well as its' readability. The cover font is "Book Antiqua". The book is perfect bound in off white pages affording it less glare (but less contrast) than pure white pages. The paper is friendly to ballpoint ink and highlighters (it is a handbook after all) and appears to handle "dog-earing" of the pages just fine. The book is printed in the U.S.A. (not China) at added expense to the Author (who doesn't mind a bit!). The book size is what's known in the industry as "Digest Size". Handy, lightweight and durable.

Like it? Order more! Joey says, "I want everyone to have access to "Divided We Fall". It's an $11.95 book, not a $20.00 or more title. A low price was important to me so that anyone could afford it. Do you have a group who would like many copies or would you like to have a sales drive to raise a little profit for your organization? Then contact me! We have discounts for bulk orders and for those trying to raise money, I'll gladly autograph you a few copies for you to auction or raffle! Whatever it takes to spread the word!"

Future plans: In 2010 we will be releasing "Divided We Fall" in large print as well as electronically for the Amazon.com "Kindle" device. Also, look for a few new titles as well as the "*We The People*" show on DVD!!

About the Author

Joey Bruno has been a technical writer and self confessed "tech" head for years. In the 90's he wrote for many magazines on the subject of computer animation and 3D graphics. He was also a speaker at several Autodesk University events on the same subjects and has taught at the college level as well. Later, based on his knowledge of business and digital imaging he became a professional photographer and has recently rededicated himself to his writing and speaking. This was rekindled by the current political state of affairs and his love and passion for America and the American people. He also loves chocolate and coffee. (He was adamant that this fact be added.)

Joey and his faithful pal "Buddy". Buddy is the one on the left.